The Word

1963–64

Writings by the Author

The Ultimate
Success Is Normal, Just Be Yourself,
  Your Eternal Identity
Fulfillment of Purpose, Volume One
Fulfillment of Purpose, Volume Two
You Are the Splendor
Gems & Poems of The Ultimate
The Gospel According to Thomas
Three Essential Steps
The Omnipresent I AM, Volume One
The Omnipresent I AM, Evidenced, Volume Two
The Ultimate Awareness, an Eternal Constant,
  Volume One
The Ultimate Awareness, an Eternal Constant,
  Volume Two
The Word 1960-1973
  (9-Volume Series)
Questions & Answers from The Word

These and other books available through:

Mystics of the World
Eliot, Maine
www.mysticsoftheworld.com

The Word

1963–64

Marie S. Watts

The Word

1963–64

by Marie S. Watts

Mystics of the World First Edition 2016
Published by Mystics of the World
ISBN-13:978-1-946362-00-1
ISBN-10: 1-946362-00-X

For information contact:

Mystics of the World
Eliot, Maine
www.mysticsoftheworld.com

Cover Graphics by Margra Muirhead
Printed by CreateSpace
Available from:

Mystics of the World.com
Amazon.com

Contents

Note to the Reader

The Word first appeared as monthly letters sent by Marie Watts to students of the Ultimate, beginning with March and ending with February of the following year.

She was at first reluctant to begin this publication, even though she sensed that it had to be done. She explains her resistance in the letter of February 1964:

> As you know, I have never wanted any personal element to enter into the activity of the Ultimate. Above all, I did not want a monthly publication to be a personal message from an assumptive leader to followers who believed that they were limited. However, one evening the title for this activity was clearly revealed; this title was so impersonal that all my reluctance dissolved, and *The Word* has been an impersonal monthly message of Truth.

Marie traveled throughout the country, giving classes and lectures. She lived constantly in a state of divine inspiration, and everything she shared flowed forth from this enlightened Consciousness. She shared these divine unfoldments in *The Word* and in her books, enabling students of the Ultimate to develop deeper understanding in specific areas and thereby rise higher in Consciousness, ultimately reaching a state of enlightenment.

From the beginning, the response from readers was one of tremendous gratitude and love. Letters came almost daily, reporting great revelation, inspiration, and so-called healing through the study and contemplation of *The Word*. She gives two reasons for this:

> Daily and nightly revelations continue increasingly in the Consciousness of the *I* that I am. But it is also true that this same revelation continues to take place increasingly as the Consciousness of the I AM that you are. … The revelations appearing in *The Word* are no more my revelations than they are *your* revelations (*The Word*, March 1962).

One reader was moved to write "A Tribute to *The Word*," which Marie included in the 1963 November issue. It reads in part:

> When *The Word* is read for the first time, there is a feeling of fullness; then, as it is reread again and again, there is no longer a reason to read anymore, but just let the Light that I am *be* the Self that I am … Be patient in your contemplations, and *The Word* will do the rest. It is a Pearl of great price. No price can be put upon it, for its value can only be revealed as you contemplate the Truth it states. *The Word* is You, *God identified*, the Christ.

Marie often expressed her great joy in witnessing the divine fulfillment of *The Word.* The deep spiritual Truth contained in these writings is indeed timeless and will be of untold value to any sincere spiritual seeker.

> We are aware that our Consciousness is boundless. We are also aware that the Consciousness of everyone is boundless. Thus, we know that anyone who is ready to perceive any specific Truth we are knowing may also perceive this same Truth.
>
> This is unselfed Love in action. This is the way in which the world must be enlightened. Above all, this is the way it is taking place. It is a glorious experience to realize that every silent contemplation is going on not only as the Consciousness of the

Identity who is contemplating, but also as the world Consciousness. It has to be this way because the Consciousness of the Identity is the world Consciousness and the Universal Consciousness (*The Word*, Dec. 1963).

March 1963

In the beginning was the Word, and the Word was with God, and the Word was God.

—John 1:1

Dear One,

Always, when I start preparing *The Word*, a great sense of sheer joyous gratitude surges and flows within and as my Consciousness. As I look out the window, the Beauty I see is so glorious that I cannot find words with which to describe It. My fingers literally fly over the keys of the typewriter, but I cannot keep my eyes on the page. There is just too much Beauty visible. The lush green of the shrubs and trees, with red berries among the green, and the beautiful flowers with their glorious and various colors are indescribable.

It keeps occurring to me that you can "tune in" visibly as well as aurally and really *see* this Beauty. Why not? The Consciousness you are is boundless, and you *can* be specifically conscious right here at any moment. You do not project your Consciousness here. It is already here, as well as where you are aware of being right this moment. When you are aware of being here, this is "here" to you, even as where you are this instant is "here" to me, if I am aware of being where you are. There is much spiritual food to be assimilated in contemplating the foregoing statements. One thing I do know: this contemplation will reveal more of your limitless, boundless Nature.

All of the foregoing came because I wished to share this Beauty with you. Suddenly it came—why not? Are you any more confined than I am confined? Of course not. Once you realize this fact, you will see this Beauty as

I see It, with the colors so much deeper and in so much greater profusion than they could appear to be if viewed by assumptive eyes of matter. So please know that you are more than welcome to "be my guest" at any moment.

Easter Sunday will be over before you receive the April issue of *The Word*. For that reason, an article on the spiritual significance of the resurrection is in order.

The following article will greatly intensify your revelation of the spiritual meaning of this glorious event. It is well that you are to receive it before Easter, in order that the Consciousness you are may be full open for the revelations which make this such a precious season.

He Is Risen

The Easter service in the churches is a beautiful ritual, even though the ritual dominates the service. For those who are enlightened, the significant Truth beyond the ritual shines through. For instance, there is always an expression of great joy and a reminder that Life is eternal and ever new. Then too, the constant newness of Life is symbolized by the recognition of the imperishable, indestructible, risen Christ.

Intrinsically, it is known that Life *is* ever new. This knowledge shows forth in so many ways, in ways that sometimes seem unimportant or downright ridiculous. Consider the practice of wearing an entirely new ensemble on Easter Sunday. Although, on the surface, this may appear to be nothing but human vanity, it actually does stem from an innate awareness of the eternal ever-newness of the Christ. Of course, we see far beyond the symbols, and they do not concern us. What does concern us is the fact that the glorious Truth does shine through, despite all the apparent inanity and vanity of assumptive man. We look for, and *see*, the spiritual *Fact* that exists despite all the illusory misinterpretation of this enduring Fact.

Let us contemplate the genuine meaning of the risen Christ. Let us perceive what was the purpose of the Resurrection. Let us discover whether or not the Christ was ever resurrected from the darkness of a tomb.

The Christ is the one indivisible Consciousness which is God. This Christ-Consciousness is conscious as the Consciousness of you, of me, and of all. It is unconfined, boundless, and indivisible. It does not divide Itself into Consciousnesses. Rather, it is omnipresent, inseparable, conscious, living Intelligence, or Mind. This unconfined Christ-Consciousness was never imprisoned within a tomb. This Christ-Consciousness was never condemned to death.

The Christ never suffered the crown of thorns, never labored under the heavy cross, and was never crucified. Who could crucify Consciousness? Who could crucify Life or Mind? Who could crucify infinite Love, the Christ-Love? *No one*. It never happened to the Christ.

The Christ-Consciousness is the enlightened Consciousness of each one of us. The darkness of the tomb can be compared to the darkness—ignorance—of any assumptive one who does not perceive himself to *be* the glorious Christ-Consciousness. Yet there is nothing conscious but Consciousness, and that which appears to be darkened consciousness—ignorance—is not really conscious at all. So the only one who is conscious *is* the Christ. To be conscious means to *be* the Christ. The risen Christ is the *only* Christ. The illumined, or enlightened, Consciousness is the *only* Consciousness.

Now the question arises: why did Jesus let it appear that he was crucified, was buried, and arose from the tomb? What was the purpose in this appearance of injustice and hate, the seeming triumph of evil? It was only an *appearance*, you know. The God-Identity they called Jesus was impervious to any such illusions. But he knew that even the illusion must *appear* to be present at the moment because *the illusion included its own obliteration.* This dispersal of the illusion was the revelation of the eternal, changeless, living Christ. *It is still the evidence of this same Christ.*

If they had but known it, the one they called Jesus was risen before they ever came to take him from the Garden of Gethsemane. It was in this same garden that the Christ-Consciousness of this glorious, loving One realized complete illumination and thus ascended to Its greatest heights. There could be no turning back for Jesus after this experience. He could no more turn back to any illusion than can infinite Mind become a petty little human mind or consciousness. Who can turn back, once he has seen and experienced being the illumined Christ-Consciousness? No one. It just can't be done. Even hatred, dishonesty, injustice, crucifixion, and a tomb are powerless to dim the enlightened Christ-Consciousness. We see all of this as just what it is: the illusion that must act as its own obliteration.

Jesus' complete illumination revealed the eternal, infinite, imperishable nature of all Life, Consciousness, Intelligence, Love. When he left the Garden of Gethsemane, he was a completely illumined Being, and he *remains* a completely illumined Identity.

Jesus' illumination revealed that there is no birth, no change, and no death. He knew that there could be no human mother, father, brother, or sister. You will remember the scene at the cross when he recognized the grief of Mary, the one they called his mother:

> Now there stood by the cross of Jesus his mother, and his mother's sister, Mary the wife of Cleophas, and Mary Magdalene. When Jesus therefore saw his mother, and the disciple standing by, whom he loved, he saith unto his mother, Woman, behold thy son! (John 19: 25-26).

It is noteworthy that Jesus did not refer to the grieving Mary as "mother." Does this sound as though Jesus believed that he had been born of human parentage? Indeed no. His complete illumination had entirely dispelled the illusion of birth. Yet he knew that birth, tragedy, and death appeared very real to the one that the world called his mother. He also knew that Mary believed him to be her son. So the Love that he was, and *is*, spoke lovingly and compassionately to her. Even so, he was revealing that genuine Love is impersonal and not to be confused with the illusory personal love which *seems* to exist in human relationships.

Yes, Jesus did perceive that there is no birth. But by that same token, he knew that there is no death. There is Bible authority for this fact. It is recorded that two thieves were also crucified when they imagined they were putting the one called Jesus to death. One of the thieves turned to Jesus and said:

> Lord, remember me when thou comest into thy kingdom. And Jesus said unto him, Verily I say unto thee, Today shalt thou be with me in paradise (Luke 23:42-43).

It is apparent from this episode that Jesus *knew* the one called a thief would not die. It is a self-evident fact that Jesus' perception that birth is an illusion would include the fact that death is but the other face of the same illusion.

It is quite generally believed that your resurrection—enlightened Consciousness—depends on your acceptance of Jesus Christ as a personal savior. Well, it doesn't. Quite the contrary. Your full illumination is your own affair. No one can give illumination to you. Neither can you "borrow" the light of another. In fact, you can't even hew your own way into illumination. It simply takes place because nothing can interfere with it, nothing can oppose it, and assuredly, nothing can stop it. The reason for this is that the fully illumined Christ-Consciousness is conscious right here and now, *as* the Consciousness you have and *are*.

Now, the question may arise: was the one they called Jesus unillumined before the night in the Garden of Gethsemane?

Jesus' words and works prior to that glorious night prove that he was illumined. In fact, had he not been illumined Christ-Consciousness, he could not have been conscious at all. He couldn't have even been alive, because Life and Consciousness are inseparably One.

Now we have arrived at the basic significance of the resurrection, namely, the *meaning* of that which has been called the Resurrection. The resurrection is the experience of full, complete illumination. But this does not mean that the Consciousness was not enlightened, or illumined, before the complete awareness of this fact was realized. There is no Consciousness other than enlightened Consciousness. Complete illumination only serves to remind us that we are illumined Consciousness. This resurrection, which *must* be experienced by each and every one of us, reveals the eternal, infinite Universe, the world, and all Existence as It *is*. Furthermore, it reveals God to *be* the *only* Universe and the only Identity.

The fact that we *are* illumined Consciousness is an eternal fact. It is evident to a greater or lesser extent in and *as* everyone in existence. But it is particularly evident as those of us who are seeing the Truth from the Absolute standpoint. We can compare our experience to the experience of the great and glorious One they called Jesus. We too *seem* to see in part, or partially, for a while, but we too finally experience the resurrection. We too seem to suffer injustice, trouble, hatred, etc., but we do reach the point of complete immunity to all such illusions. We too appear to be crucified, but we know that the crucifixion is only an illusion's own picturization of itself. We too seem to experience our night in the Garden of Gethsemane, but we walk as completely illumined Beings from that point on. We too come to know that there is no birth, no change, and no death. We even find ourselves saying, "I am the way, the truth, and the life" (John 14:6).

Yes, beloved, "The night is far spent, the day is at hand" (Rom. 13:12). We have "cast off the darkness," and we have "put on the armor of light." We know that the eternal Life we *are* can never be born or die. We know that the infinite Light we *are* can never be extinguished in the darkness of a tomb. We know that complete illumined Consciousness is our Consciousness, right here and now, and we know that each day we are more aware of this fact. If we *seem* to have been the crucified ones, we can rejoice in the fact that we are also the resurrected ones.

The one called Jesus was not alone in the Garden of Gethsemane. Neither was he alone in the Resurrection. His experience is also our experience. Not that he did it *for* us. Oh no! He didn't even go through this experience in order to leave an example for us or to prove anything *to* us. He simply went through whatever was necessary for each one of us to experience. But he never seemed to be as deeply involved in the illusion as most of us have seemed to be. Yet even this wonderfully illumined one did not realize that he was completely illumined Consciousness until the Gethsemane experience.

So it is with us. We continue right on, regardless of the many *appearances* of evil, and we have our resurrection in our own Garden of Gethsemane. It is truly a glorious experience. Now we walk as completely illumined Beings, entirely untouched by any illusion of a presence or a power other than God. God *is truly* All. All *is truly* God. We see it, we know it, we *are* it. We are the risen Christ that endureth forevermore. We are the risen Christ that is alive forever, and we are the one inextinguishable Light that is Life. We are the resurrection and the Life, for we know ourselves to be the *one* infinite, eternal Self.

This is what Easter means to us. It means the ever newness of eternal, perfect, living, loving, conscious Intelligence. And it reminds us that *we are this ever new, eternal, perfect, living, loving, conscious Intelligence right here and now. There is neither space nor time in which we can be other than that which we are.*

Of Purer Eyes

There is a most profound statement in our Bible, and it is fraught with power. Of course, there are many, many profound statements in this great book, and they are all powerful. But I know of no other single short statement that has revealed omnipresent Perfection so quickly and so often as has the following:

> Thou art of purer eyes than to behold evil, and canst not look on iniquity (Hab. 1:13).

Of course, this statement of Habakkuk, if not spiritually perceived, would mean very little, and certain it is that it would not reveal the Perfection that *is*. So let us perceive just what it is in this pure, powerful revelation that is so profound and so powerful. Furthermore, let us discover just why it so often reveals the Perfection which does exist.

It is true, God cannot see, know, or be evil. But this would not help us very much if *we* continued to see, know, and be the illusion called evil. God is pure Absolute Truth. This means that God is "free from imperfection, complete in its own character, perfect, whole, free from mixture, free from limit or qualification." The definition is from Webster's Unabridged Dictionary. This definition of the Absolute is certainly the Absolute Truth, and God *is* the Absolute Truth. Furthermore, the Absolute Truth is God.

God is complete Perfection, complete as Itself, complete Wholeness, and completely free from limits or qualifications of any kind.

Why is it that God "is of purer eyes than to behold evil"? God is All. Being All, God can only behold Itself. God can only be aware of what God *is*. But it is important to realize that God is aware of *being* what God eternally and infinitely is. Being limitless, unqualified, unconditioned Perfection, God can only be conscious of Perfection. Being All, and being free from any mixture with anything other than Itself, God can only be aware of Its pure, uncontaminated Entirety. Being boundless and immeasurable, God cannot be aware of anything outside of, or other than, Itself. So, as stated before, God can only behold Itself.

It is well to consider the following fact: God *is* that which God beholds. God is that which God sees, that which God knows, and that which God experiences. This has to be true, for there is nothing but God for God to see, know, or be. It follows, then, that God must ever behold His own immutable Perfection, His own uncontaminated Purity, His own unqualified, unconditioned, limitless, boundless Nature.

If God were to behold evil, He would have to *be* the evil which He beheld, for God *is* All. If God were to know impurity, He would have to be the impurity which He knew, for All *is* God. If God were to know or experience bondage, God would have to be in bondage to Himself, for there is none other than God. If God were to be incomplete, He would have to be His own incompleteness. If God were to be limited or bounded in any way, He would have to be His own limitation, His own boundary, for there is nothing that is not God.

Yes, God can only see Himself, know Himself, and be what He sees and knows. Being All, God is the *only*

One who beholds, the *only* One who knows, and the *only* One who exists. Thus, all Existence consists of God seeing, knowing, and being just what God *is*. There is no one to see but God. There is no one to know but God. There is no one to *be* but God. There is nothing to be seen but God. There is nothing to know but God, and there is nothing to *be* but God.

Now, you exist. This much you *know*. You are conscious; thus, you are conscious of the fact that you exist. You can know that you exist only because you are conscious. God is the *only* Consciousness, so God is the only Consciousness of existing. Your consciousness of existing is God, being aware of *being Itself*. Do you see what this means? It means that you can know nothing of yourself. It means that your very consciousness of existing is but God being conscious of being Itself and that it is impossible for *you* to know anything that is unknown to God.

Actually, there is no evil. That which appears to be evil is nothing but illusion. If one appears to see, know, or experience evil, that one would have to be deluded. But God is not deluded, so there is no one deluded. This means that a seemingly deluded one is the same illusion which constitutes the evil that appears to be seen, known, and experienced. An illusion is nothing; God is All. A deluded one is nothing; All is God. But *you are something*, and this Something is just what God is and nothing else.

You see that which is here to be seen, and you are the pure, uncontaminated Vision which beholds no evil. You know that which exists to be known, and you are the pure Consciousness, without a taint of evil, which is completely unconscious of evil. You are Something, and you are the pure, unfettered, boundless, conscious, living, loving Intelligence which is God. So you, knowing anything, have to be constituted of God, knowing that which God knows.

How, then, can you know evil? How, then, can you see or be evil? You can't. You aren't.

There is no use denying that evil seems very real. To deny this *appearance* of evil would be ridiculous. But Jesus did not judge by appearance. "Judge not according to the appearance, but judge righteous judgment" (John 7:24). If Jesus had judged by the appearance, he would have judged Lazarus to be dead. If he had judged by the appearance, he would have considered Mary Magdalene to be a hopeless sinner, one who deserved to be punished. Suppose he had accepted the appearance of leprosy, of blindness, of epilepsy; suppose he had accepted the appearance of imperfection of any kind, If he had accepted the appearance of evil, would he have been able to reveal Perfection, eternal Life, pure bodies, etc? Indeed no!

Jesus too was of purer eyes than to behold evil, because he had realized his God-Identity. The Vision that is pure does not actually see impurity or evil of any kind.

There is a verse in our Bible which is rarely quoted or written. I have often wondered why it has not attracted more attention:

> Unto the pure all things are pure, but unto them that are defiled and unbelieving is nothing pure; but even their mind and conscience is defiled (Titus 1:15).

Yes, when the Consciousness really is enlightened, we are not deluded by any appearance of evil. We too are of purer eyes than to behold evil.

Jesus made one very revealing statement which really pertains to any appearance of evil:

> Get thee behind me, Satan: thou art an offense unto me: for thou savourest not the things that be of God, but those that be of men (Matt. 16:23).

This statement is truly significant. Jesus refused to look at or see evil. He knew that the "things of God" are not evil. He also knew that All *is* God and that there can be nothing that is not God being that thing. He was fully aware of the fact that anything that appears to be evil can only *appear* as evil to the assumptive mind of man. In short, he knew that the Mind which is God knows the things of God, while the mind of illusory man must know only the illusions of this illusory man.

Now, you must wonder how this knowledge can be practical. It may seem too much like a beautiful theory to be your experience in these so-called days of trouble and strife. But is it? Let us examine this revelation somewhat and see why it is true and why it proves itself to be practical in everyday living and experience.

First of all, it was quite practical when Lazarus came walking out of the tomb. It was a proven Truth when the blind received their sight, the lame walked, and the lepers were revealed to be pure. It was no less practical when Mary Magdalene was completely freed from guilt, punishment, and shame. Oh yes, it was proven to be practical by Jesus.

This same Truth is proving to be practical today in the Life and Experience of many students of the Ultimate. Let us perceive just why it should be so powerful in our lives.

Let us go back to our basic Principle: if God cannot know evil, it is impossible for you to know it. You cannot actually see evil without knowing it. You are the Consciousness which is unaware of evil.

Suppose, for instance, it seemed that you saw an evil person. As far as you were concerned, that evil person would be in your Consciousness because you would be conscious of him. Now, you would ask your Self: is God aware of an evil person or evil of any nature? Of course not. Then is God aware of a person capable of being other than Itself? No! Then God cannot know either the person or the evil. If God knows it not, you cannot know it, for you have no mind of your own, separate from, or other than, the Mind that is God. As you contemplate this Truth, you will find that the illusion called evil persons will fade away. In its place, you will discover God, the All, and the only Identity you can know is God identified.

Now suppose you seem to be experiencing pain. Certain it is that if pain were genuine, it would have to be evil. Here again, you would ask: does God know this pain? Is God conscious of it? Is God aware of experiencing this suffering? Most important of all: is God aware of *being* either the pain or the sufferer? Ah, there is the great Truth to be realized.

God is not conscious of illness. God could not be in pain, neither could God be suffering with pain. Only what God knows can God experience. Only what God knows and experiences being, can you know and experience being. Therefore, you cannot experience being in pain. In other words, *you know it not*. If pain existed in your experience, you certainly would know it. But if you "know it not," it can have no existence in or as your Universe, your experience, or your Body.

Beloved, you can actually see this Truth evidenced in every experience of your daily Life. When you see as God sees, you are going to see what God sees. When you hear as God hears, you are going to hear what God hears. When you experience as God experiences, you are going to experience what God experiences.

Now you can say to any appearance of evil, "God knows it not; thus, I know it not. God sees it not; thus, I see it not. God hears it not; thus, I hear it not. God experiences it not; thus, I experience it not. What God knows, I know. What God sees, I see. What God hears, I hear. What God experiences, I experience. And above all, what God *is*, I am."

Questions and Answers

Q: What is man?

A: That which is generally considered to be man is an illusion's illusion. This fact was brought out in the February 1962 issue of *The Word.* We are cognizant of the fact that birth is an illusion and that Life, Consciousness, Mind are eternal.

We are not the first to realize that birth is not a reality. In our Bible there are several references to Melchizedek, who was referred to as being "without father, without mother, without descent, having neither beginning of days, nor end of life, but made like unto the Son of God, abideth a priest continually" (Heb. 7:3).

This is a genuine portrayal of you, of me, and of everyone. We know that the Father and the Son are the same Consciousness, Intelligence, Life; thus, the so-called Son must be as birthless and as deathless as is the One called Father.

If we say there is no person, we are speaking Truth. If we say there is no Identity, we are speaking falsehood. The Infinity which is God identifies Itself as innumerable aspects of Itself. That which is called man is but an illusion *about* the eternal Identity which is God identified. Yet there *is* Something here which is miscalled man. The misconception about that which is here cannot change the fact that God, identified, does exist. Furthermore, God, identified as you and as me, is distinctly identified as that aspect of Itself which is *misconceived* to be man. There is a distinction between God as Man and God as Tree, Bird, or whatever. There is distinction, but there is no division. God *identifies* Itself, but God does not divide Itself.

The one they called Jesus was, and is, the Christ. The Christ is that distinct aspect of God which *we* call man.

The Christ is eternal. The Christ is comprised of conscious, perfect, living, loving Intelligence. The Christ is indivisible from God, for the Christ *is* God in Essence, in Activity, and in *Form*. Remember, though, the Christ in Form does not divide God into gods. The Christ, as the Body of you and the Body of me, is unconfined and unconfinable.

The misconception of that which is called man is due to our misconception of Body. Once we really see and *know* what constitutes the Body, we will be fully aware of our Christ-Consciousness, our Christ-Love, our Christ-Mind, Christ-Life, and our Christ-Body. The Christ-Body is the Body of Light, which is spoken of in the Bible. This Body is never seen as solid, confined substance. Rather, It is perceived as delineated Light, yet the delineation does not confine the Light.

Oh, if there were only words with which to tell you that which you alone must experience. My Heart yearns to tell all of it to you. But I know it is futile to try. One thing I know: there *is* a distinct Identity right here where a misidentity appears to be. This distinct Identity is God being You, being Me, being Everyone. This glorious Identity which is here does reveal one aspect of Itself as Body. But this Body is far from being anything like the born body of assumptive man.

I can tell you that man as such does not really exist. But I must also say that *you, as an Identity, do exist*. You exist eternally, without change and without interruption. Many of you have already experienced seeing and *being* the Body of Light, which is God in Essence. Those of you who have not had this glorious experience *will* experience *being* the Christ as Life, as Consciousness, as Intelligence, as Love, and as Body.

God *is* All. To be All means to be complete. If anything were to be missing from the All, then the Entirety which is God would not be All. In other words, God would be incomplete. The Completeness which is God consists of innumerable aspects of Itself. Each aspect of the Infinitude which is God is that specific Identity and no other. Yet God is the *only* Identity. No specific aspect of the infinite Identity can be missing. Neither can there be one extraneous aspect included in the Completeness which is God. The Infinite All consists of *only* that which is essential to Its infinite completeness, perfection, and eternal, harmonious activity. That which is called man is absolutely essential to the Completeness which is God, to the Perfection which is God, and to the completely perfect Activity which is God in action.

No one can deny that the Christ was actively fulfilling a definite purpose as the activity of the one they called Jesus. The Christ is the genuine and only Identity of each and every one of us. Let us know that *our activity is the definite fulfillment of a purpose that is essential to the completeness which is God*. It may appear that our activity is unimportant at the moment. But there is no activity that is unimportant to the complete Omniaction which is God. Your activity is the evidence of the fact that God is Omniaction. Your Identity is the evidence of the fact that God *is*. Without You, the infinite, omnipresent, omniactive Identity which is God would not be complete. But You exist. I exist. Each and every Identity does exist. Thus, the infinite All is eternally, omniactively complete.

Our beloved Bible says:

> Cease ye from man, whose breath is in his nostrils: for wherein is he to be accounted of? (Isa. 2:22).

Let us cease the acceptance or recognition of "man with breath in his nostrils." Let us perceive that there is no accounting for this illusory concept of man. Let us discard completely the manhood and accept the Christhood of our Identity. Let us absolve our Christ-Identity from any illusion called man and accept *only* the glory of the *risen* Christ.

Indeed the Christ is risen *as* You. No assumptive mortal can usurp the Identity of the risen Christ that You *are*. You do not have to *become* the Christ-Identity which you already are. You need not even struggle to become aware of your Christ-Identity. Your only necessity is to recognize and accept your glorious Christhood. Thus, you will no longer question about nonexistent man. Rather, you will discover that you *are* the very Christ you have recognized and accepted. You will walk in and as the Light you *are*, and you will know that the risen Christ is your *only* Life, Mind, Consciousness, Love, Being, and Body. This, beloved, is your Identity. Rejoice and be exceedingly glad, for your names are eternally written in heaven.

The Risen Christ

The risen Christ is ever here,
Impervious to "far" and "near,"
The ever present Light;
The risen Christ remains the same,
To lift the blind, the halt, the lame,
Above illusion's blight.

The wondrous, loving, living One,
The Light far greater than the sun,
So infinite, so pure;
Is here as You, so glorious
As your own Life, victorious,
Which ever doth endure.

Light and Love,
Marie S. Watts

April 1963

In the beginning was the Word, and the Word was with God, and the Word was God.

—John 1:1

Dear One,

There is much news to share with you in this issue of *The Word*. All of it is good, of course. The activities of the Ultimate are moving faster and faster. In fact, they are moving so rapidly that sometimes I am literally awed at the pace. It is wonderful to realize that I do not propel these activities. I am simply carried along with them, often as a leaf is carried along by a good brisk breeze. In any event, I am joyously, freely busy, and it is a wonderfully satisfying activity.

Our class in San Francisco was a beautiful experience. Those of you who attended already know that the revelations were tremendous and enlightening. Many of you "tuned in," and your reports are proof beyond doubt that you were experiencing many of the revelations which we were privileged to experience. All of us can be assured of one fact: the enlightened Consciousness of those who attended was responsible for the tremendous revelations we shared during that class. If the members of the class, as a unit, had not been so greatly enlightened, the revelations would not have been so complete and so inspiring.

As you know, the Ultimate can never be organized. This is the way of complete freedom, and organization always tends to restrict. Then, too, an organization must also have a leader, and there can be no leader in this approach. Each one is his own leader, his own master. This is the only way the Ultimate can fulfill its purpose of being impersonal Truth–and Truth is impersonal.

However, there have been many requests for information about meetings for those interested in the Ultimate. These requests have come from those of you who wish to be entirely free from dualism and wish to attend meetings in which only the Absolute pure Truth is presented. You have stated that you do not wish to search any longer through the chaff of dualistic statements for the grain of pure Truth. I can understand this, because I know that most of you have, as I have, come all the way down the long road of dualism.

The question has been, how can we have these meetings in which the pure Absolute is presented and still remain completely free of organization and leadership? For every question there is an answer, and the answer to this question is here revealed. Above all, complete freedom must be maintained, for freedom is a basic principle of the Ultimate. For this reason, I have never interfered in any way with the presentation of the Ultimate at meetings being held throughout the country, and rarely have I mentioned, even in private correspondence, where these meetings were being held or by whom they were being conducted.

Your requests for this information have been so numerous that it is apparent there is a way in which it is supplied. So from time to time, in *The Word*, you will be informed about these meetings and by whom they are being conducted. I feel confident that only the pure Absolute Truth will be presented during these meetings where students of the Ultimate are completely One in Consciousness.

Frequently I am asked the following questions: "What about those who are still in dualism but who wish to know more about the Ultimate? Wouldn't it be better to make some compromise and lead them out of dualism gradually, by mixing a certain amount of dualism with the Absolute?"

Of course, each one is free to speak or to read whatever seems right to him at the moment. But dualism and the Absolute will not mix. The word *Ultimate* has come to mean the pure Absolute to most of you. So when a meeting is being conducted under the title of the Ultimate, it would be better to keep it completely free from duality. Those who are ready for the pure Absolute will continue to attend the meetings. Those who are not will drop away, and will, as they should, return to a more dualistic approach.

Fortunately, there are numerous organizations in which these sincere seekers may continue their search. In keeping with the basic Principle of the Ultimate, it is right to "loose them, and let them go," completely free. Only in complete freedom can they discover their free, perfect, boundless, God-Identity. Let us rejoice in the fact that there are organized religions and groups through which they may find whatever is necessary for their particular needs at the moment. But let us not try to usurp the prerogative of those who are helping them right where they seem to be.

Our activity in the Ultimate is not to try to bring anyone out of dualism; rather, it is simply to present the pure, untainted Absolute Truth, complete in Its own purity. We are completely unconcerned by the members who attend, or do not attend, our meetings. Our only concern is to keep the presentation of the Ultimate Absolute free from any taint of dualism. By leaving each one completely free to discover his own Identity, we have freed ourselves from any illusion of leadership. Thus, we are free from all personal sense, which means we are free from dualism ourselves.

Now, occasionally, I will have a report that someone claims to be teaching the Ultimate who is actually teaching dualism. Generally, I have not previously heard of this one and have no way of knowing what he or she is presenting. Rarely do I have a report that anyone who has attended classes in the Ultimate presents anything that is dualistic. When this has been the case, it is due to a sincere desire to bridge the gap between duality and the Absolute.

However, some of you have asked me what should be done about those who are presenting dualism under the name of the Ultimate. I can only say, I am not a master or a leader. I do consider that it is vitally important to keep the presentation completely Absolute, so long as it is done under the banner of the Ultimate. Yet I must leave everyone free. For this reason, I cannot tell you what to do. The decision must be entirely within your own Consciousness. If you feel that you can sift all the chaff from the wheat in these presentations, and that you are being enlightened by attending them, by all means follow your own sincere inclinations. But above all, "to thine own self be true." This is all that matters. This is all that concerns you or me. There can be no autocracy in the Ultimate.

The new book, *You Are the Splendor*, is almost ready for the publisher. There are a few more pages to be added and the final editing to be done. I have no words to tell you how I feel about this book. I can only say that it is the answer to much that has seemed to be unclear in the Absolute, and It is going to fulfill a tremendously important purpose. I have felt a surging, omniactive impulsion throughout the entire revelation of this living Light, and I know that you will experience this same glorious impulsion in reading it.

The Unbroken Circle

We have written and we have talked about the irrepressible, surging activity which we have called Omniaction. Many of us have experienced the conscious Presence of this rhythmic, surging activity. So let us now explore this experience and perceive more of its spiritual significance.

It has been said by physicists that there is no such thing as a straight line in nature. We know that if we were to attempt a flight to Mars, we could never arrive at our destination if we flew in a straight line. We would have to first circle the Earth planet and then fly in ever expanding circles until we reached that point where we would naturally descend to the planet Mars.

There are innumerable ways in which the significance of circular activity is apparent. For instance, if one is supposed to be lost in a wilderness or in a desert, he will inevitably return to his starting point, even though he imagines he has been walking in a straight line, away from his original area. It has been said that the planes orbit in circles, and we can be quite sure that this circular activity is an omnipresent fact throughout the entire Universe.

A circle may appear to be small, or it may appear to be tremendous. Yet a circle remains a circle, and the activity is the same Omniaction. Therefore, we can confidently say that this circular, rhythmic Omniaction is a universal Fact. Let us not be deceived here; this does not mean that the Universe is bounded by a circumference. God is the Universe, and God is boundless Infinity. Nonetheless, universal, omnipresent Omniaction does reveal Itself as a flowing, circular, rhythmic activity.

A circle is a symbol of Completeness. This is the spiritual significance of the rhythmic, surging activity we realize and experience. A circle is without beginning and without ending. The beginning and the ending are the same. This is clearly brought out by the one they called Jesus in *The Gospel According to Thomas*. Without quoting, let us remind ourselves that he said, in substance, "Where the beginning is, there is also the ending."

The circle must be unbroken if it is to be a perfect circle. So there can be no interruption to eternal Existence. There can be no break in the unbroken circle of eternal Perfection. This is true of Life, Intelligence, Consciousness, and Love. There can be no interruption in the beginningless, changeless, endless, living, intelligent, conscious Love which comprises the entirety of every Identity.

If there could be a beginning or an ending, the circle would be broken. If there could be birth and death, there would be an interruption in the complete circle. Thus, there would be an interruption of the eternal, infinite omniaction which is Life. This would mean incompleteness, and there is no such thing as an incomplete God.

Let us remind ourselves right here that God is the Universe. The Universe is God. If there is no birth, God is not a creator. If God were a creator, God would also be a destroyer, for anything that is created begins. Anything that has beginning must also come to an end. But God does not create. Neither does God destroy. If Life could begin and end, God Itself would have to have a beginning and ending, for God is Life. If Life could be interrupted or disrupted, God Itself would have to be interrupted or disrupted.

The complete circle denotes the Completeness which is God, the Universe. The complete circle denotes the Completeness which is *you.* Do you see what this means? It means that you are complete as All that is God. The Life you are is complete, eternal, infinite. The Consciousness you are is eternally, infinitely complete. The intelligent Love you are is uninterrupted by birth or by death. The eternal Perfection you are is uninterrupted by a period of imperfection. The complete Perfection you are knows no vacuum in Its Perfection, no lapse in Its Consciousness of being perfect, and no lapse in Its perfect activity. The complete Love you are knows no lapse into hatred, animosity, or criticism. The complete Love you are knows no vacuums, no area in which Its completeness is not entire. The complete Love you are knows no presence that can defy or defile Its purity. You cannot be made to dislike, to ridicule, or to condemn anyone. There is no such thing as hatred or condemnation in the Completeness which you are.

Complete Life must, of necessity, be eternal Life. By Its very nature, It must be without beginning or ending. If there could be a lapse or an interruption in Life, It would not be complete. This is why there can be no temporal Life. A temporal Life would be an incomplete Life, and Life is God—Completeness. All that is true of Life is true of Consciousness. This is true because Intelligence, Love, Life, Consciousness are one integral Whole.

Omniaction is indivisibly present as One Life, Consciousness, Intelligence, Love. There is no inactive Life, Mind, Consciousness, or Intelligence. If there were such a thing as inactivity, there would be no Life, no Mind, no Consciousness, and no Love. But there *is* activity, and it is omnipresent.

This is a complete Universe, and all that is essential to Its completeness exists eternally, in and *as* the infinite All. God, the Universe, is Perfection. So this is a completely perfect Universe. If there could be the slightest flaw, this would not be a perfect Universe. If there could be even so much as an infinitesimal dot of imperfection, we could not say that God, the Universe, was completely perfect. Thus, Perfection is a Universal Fact. It is equally present everywhere and eternally.

All of the foregoing is true, but there is something that must be realized if it is to be evident in our daily affairs, in our homes, and in our bodies: we must be *completely conscious* of the *Entirety* which constitutes infinite Perfection.

We cannot deny that imperfection appears to be present. Sometimes it seems that we are more aware of imperfection than we are of Perfection. Certain it is that every effort seems to be made to call our attention to the *appearance* of imperfection. If we are accepting this phantasmic appearance as genuine, we are not fully aware of the infinite, eternal Fact. Perfection is the Fact. Imperfection is not a Fact. Every Truth in existence is an eternal, infinite Truth. Any *appearance* of imperfection must have a beginning and an ending. Thus, this illusion cannot be genuine. It is not an eternal Fact.

Now, if perfection is to be the *only* Fact present in and *as* your experience, you must be conscious *only* of this Fact. Of course, it is the Fact, whether or not you seem to be aware of it. But you may ask, "How am I going to steadfastly see Perfection when imperfection keeps intruding into my affairs, my body, and my experience?" Ah, right here is where omniactive Consciousness must be realized. Furthermore, right here is where the irresistible surge of infinite Intelligence must be perceived.

Consciousness is active. If It were not, It could not be alive, and Consciousness is inseparable from Life. The activity of your conscious perception is your completely perfect Consciousness in action. The Consciousness that is completely perfect can only be conscious of Perfection. The activity of your *only* Consciousness, and the *only* activity of your Consciousness, is the active perception of complete Perfection.

Beloved, contemplate this Truth. Let it abide within and *as* your Consciousness. If you will do this, you will find false evidence of imperfection disappearing from your experience. Know what constitutes your Consciousness—God. Know what constitutes the activity of your Consciousness—God. Know what constitutes the completeness of your Consciousness and the completeness of Its activity—

God. Recognize the infinite, irrepressible, omniactive surge to be your Consciousness in action. Realize that you can have no existence other than this infinite, complete, surging, living, loving, intelligent Consciousness.

Oh, there is more, much more, I would share with you on this word *Completeness*. But all that I could tell you is already present—and consciously present—as your own Consciousness. Let It surge. Let It gently, lovingly flow in, through, and *as* your entire Being. Let It be. It already is. Just be "full open" and let there be no illusory obstacles to your full and complete revelation.

Consider the symbol of the circle. Consider the infinite, eternal significance of this symbol. There is no end to the revelation which can be experienced as you abide in the contemplation of this glorious, complete, omniactive Universe. Truly, God *is* All, All *is* God. Truly, God *is* Love, Love *is* God. And so it is. Let it be, for it is your God-Self.

Ye Ask Amiss

> Ye ask, and receive not, because ye ask amiss, that ye may consume it upon your lusts (James 4:3).

If we were to interpret the foregoing verse from the standpoint of orthodoxy, it would certainly appear to be dualistic. Not only that, it would make one uncertain as to what to pray for and what not to pray for. However, if, as enlightened Consciousness, you perceive the deeper spiritual significance of this verse, it becomes vitally alive with meaning. Let us examine this statement from the standpoint of the Ultimate.

James had walked and talked with the one they called Jesus. He must have known that prayer was not a petition to God for something. Surely he must have perceived the

Omnipresence of God. So his genuine meaning must have been far different than is the generally accepted concept of this statement from the Book of James.

What does it mean to "ask amiss"? It means to be mistaken in our concept of prayer. It means that we do not understand the true meaning of prayer. So let us begin by a consideration of just what it means to pray.

What is prayer? And, for that matter, to whom do we pray? Prayer, as we understand it, is a holy experience. It takes place when we are consciously in the "holy of holies" and there is no assumptive little "I" pretending to be something.

Actually, true prayer is experienced when we want nothing. Of course, it is not a matter of asking for anything. It is not even a hope or a desire for something which prompts us to be consciously full open in prayer. If we seem to be asking for something, or even if we seem to be desiring something, we are not really in conscious prayer.

James says, "Ye ask, and receive not," and then he goes on and explains just why prayer is apparently unanswered. The prayer that carries within it any least plea for human satisfaction, help, or even healing is a prayer of dualism. It is small wonder that so often the prayer is unanswered. In fact, the wonder is that it is ever answered at all. And when it is, the answer is due to a sincere and intense faith in God. It is true that sometimes our faith is so great and our Love so boundless that we do experience being the Presence, even though we may not understand this at the moment. When this takes place, we experience what is called a healing or have what is sometimes called a demonstration. But too often, we seem to have been too engrossed with an appearance of trouble or inharmony to really completely forget the little "I" that imagines it wants something for itself.

Those of us who are seeing from a standpoint of the Ultimate know better than to ask for anything. We know there is no God outside our own Being to whom we can pray. But if we are not constantly alert, we too are capable of falling into the trap of dualism. When this takes place, we wonder why we are not seeing and experiencing the evidence of the Absolute Truth we so sincerely accept and believe.

Let us state one example of this apparent failure to experience the evidence of that which we know to be true. Many of you have had the following experience or one similar to it. You may seem to have more than one problem. In fact, it may appear that your problems are many. Yet there is always one specific problem that seems more important than any of the others. Often you will say that you know "if only this one big problem can be solved, the others will disappear." The paradox is that frequently the so-called other problems will disappear one by one, and you hardly notice that they are gone. Yet that one big important difficulty will seem to remain.

Now, why is this true? The answer to this question is that "ye ask amiss." In other words, you have been able to obliterate the assumptive little "I" where the lesser problems were concerned, but your attention was focused on the one important appearance of "otherness." Thus, you still seemed to experience the appearance of inharmony which concerned the assumptive little self.

Now, Perfection is normal. It is natural and right to expect Perfection to be realized and evidenced. But to desire or even hope for Perfection is to assume that It is not already present in and as your own Being. In short, even as you apparently wish for Perfection, you are denying that you already have It because *you are It*. If you hope for Perfection, you are assuming that It is not present now but that It will appear sometime in either the near or the far future.

We do not seek anything. We do not attempt to change anything or to bring anything to pass. Our necessity is not to be freed from anything and not to have anything added to us. Rather, it is to consciously *know* God. To consciously know God is to be conscious of the perfect Self. But this Consciousness must be realized through a complete relinquishment of all assumptive human desires, wishes, or hopes. This is true prayer, and it is illumined, conscious perception.

Illumined, conscious Perception is Perfection perceived and manifested right here and now. It is the perception that Perfection *is* because God is Perfection and God is All.

Illumined, conscious Perfection cannot be realized or evidenced so long as we appear to be burdened with a false sense of problems. You see, it is the little nonexistent "I" that seems to have the problem. It is impossible for the assumptive little "I" to be or to become illumined. Non-intelligence does not become Intelligence. Non-intelligence must ever remain just what it is, and it is not Mind, or an absence of Mind. It is not until we perceive the Omnipresence which *is* Mind that illumined, conscious Perfection can be experienced and manifested.

> And my soul shall be joyful in the Lord: it shall rejoice in his salvation (Ps. 35:9).

The Soul, Consciousness, that is enlightened is a joyous Consciousness. It is never burdened. Rather, It is ever free, joyous, and inspired. Our Bible abounds in numerous references to joy. We cannot carry a problem-burdened, assumptive mind into the Consciousness which is the Presence. It is necessary to relinquish the seeming burden, or problem, first. Then we can joyously, freely realize that we are in the Presence because we *are* the Presence.

Sometimes a problem appears to be so great and so real that it seems impossible to be oblivious to it. I know all about this, and I understand it. But I have learned that it is possible to free yourself from *any* false appearance, no matter how serious, worrisome, or painful it may appear to be. Let me share with you a way that has been most helpful in my own experience.

First of all, I am always aware that of myself I can do nothing, know nothing, be nothing. I do not use these words as a formula. Rather, it is just a quiet relinquishment of all personal sense of being anything. I abide in this quiet non-selfed humility until the glorious, flowing, surging Light is seen, felt, experienced, and known to be the entirety of the Universe. It is now clear that God—the Light—is the whole of me, the All of All, the All *as* All.

However, there is one aspect of this approach that must be realized: this realization takes place during the relinquishment of the little assumptive "I." I ask for nothing. I seek nothing. I do not "put off the old man with his deeds" with *any* object in mind. I rejoice in the fact that God *is* All. My Heart sings in the realization that All *is* God. And above all, I love.

Oh, beloved One, Love is the great answer. Conscious Love is the obliteration of the offensive little "I." In conscious Love, the seeming problem disappears. In conscious Love, there is ecstatic joy. In conscious Love, there is God and God alone, for God *is* Love. So let the Mind that is Love be your Mind.

If it seems at the moment that you just can't love, *don't you believe it*. You can't exist unless Love is the very Essence and activity of your Existence. If it is difficult to experience this great surge of impersonal Love, consider a beautiful flower. You can always love the beauty of a flower. You can always love Beauty. Loving Beauty, you are loving God, for God is Beauty. Loving Beauty, you are loving everyone and everything. Loving Beauty, you are loving your Self, for God *is* your Self.

Of one thing you can be certain: you can never ask amiss so long as your Heart, Being, Soul, and Body are Love-filled. Infinite, impersonal Love is completely unselfed Love. To love is to rejoice. So love always, all the way, that you may rejoice all the way. Thus, your perfect God-Identity is revealed all ways.

Questions and Answers

Q: What about the birds during the cold winter months? I warm food for them, and before they can eat much of it, the food has frozen solid.

A: Compassion is a wonderful thing, for compassion is Love. Of course we always act lovingly and compassionately. Yet even as we perform these loving acts, there must be an awareness of the Truth of any situation.

All that appears in form in the phantasmic world of materiality is subject to the trouble, the pains, and the struggle of this fictitious appearance. Of course, there can also seem to be pleasant and harmonious experiences in this world of fantasy. But whether these experiences appear to be good or bad, they are not genuine experiences at all. You will remember the mockingbird that flew against our window with such violence that it seemed to die. You will also remember the glorious evidence of eternal, perfect Life that was apparent when this transpired. Let us compare the body of the mockingbird with the bodies of the birds that seem to suffer so greatly during the cold winter months.

Was the Body of the mockingbird the *appearance* of its body, which seemed to suffer an accident and to die? No! The Body of the mockingbird was the eternal Body that was not injured and could not die. It was the perfect, free, joyous Body that I saw fly into the atmosphere with a song in its Heart.

Thus it is with the Bodies of birds, animals, trees, flowers, or whatever. Thus it is with the Bodies of you and of me. The eternal Body of Light is not subject to cold, heat, or hunger. It is not subject to the beliefs of nonexistent substance, activity, or form. It is Self-sustaining and Self-maintaining, needing nothing to make It more complete, more perfect, or more eternal than It is.

The Body of the bird is comprised of the Consciousness which is the bird. It knows nothing of either heat or cold. It knows nothing of the pangs of hunger or the satisfaction of appetite. It knows nothing of suffering. It is free from pain. It is consciously perfect, harmonious, immutable, and eternal. In fact, the Body of the bird is constituted of the same conscious, living, loving Mind that constitutes the Body of you and of me. Therefore, the Consciousness of the bird and the Consciousness of you or me is the very same Consciousness. The Essence of the bird is the very same Essence as is the substance of the Body of you or of me.

I Know I Am

I only know I Am,
What other could I know?
'Tis falsity and sham
That just pretends to show
Another being, separate,
In darkness and in fear,
A being, oh so desperate,
Not knowing *I* am here.

If darkness, fear, and doubt,
Abideth here to flout
The only *I* 'tis strange,
I know it not, nor aught of change;
Oh, if another, there could be
In darkness, sickness, pain,
How could the One I AM be he?
Doth not the *I* remain?

No matter how he may appear,
I see him perfect, pure,
The everlasting Light so clear,
As Light, he must endure
As All I am, not separate
In terms of time or space,
Not troubled, worried, desperate,
But living as my Grace.

As Love, as Truth, as boundless Life,
He lives in joyous peace,
Beyond delusion's strife,
He finds complete release.

Light and Love,
Marie S. Watt

May 1963

In the beginning was the Word, and the Word was with God, and the Word was God.

—John 1:1

Dear One,

Thank you so very much for your many letters expressing appreciation for the new format of *The Word*. We are happy with it also, and we know that it will continue to improve.

It is my hope that our next issue of *The Word* will bring more news of the new book, *You Are the Splendor*. In fact, we may know the approximate time of its publication. There! I did it. I used the word *time*. And yet there is no time. Nonetheless, I know you will be happy to know that it is finished and that I am happy with it.

Actually, as I read it, I am awed by it because it is so apparent that no little person named Marie could have written it. I know that you will feel the same way about it when you read it. Of one thing I am certain: the revelations presented in this new book are pure Consciousness fulfilling a glorious Purpose, and the Consciousness which revealed Itself as this book is aware of Its purpose and Its fulfillment. Most important of all is the fact that every Truth revealed throughout its pages is already eternally established within and as your own Consciousness.

You will not find anyone named Marie S. Watts in this book. In fact, you will find no one other than your own God-Identity. You will recognize your Self in the Truths this book reveals, and it is in this way that it fulfills its purpose. To find God means to recognize your Self. To find your Self means to recognize God. And who else is there to find or to recognize? There is One alone to discover, to know, and to be—and this One is God. This One God is your own Identity. When all fallacious sense of a little "I" is obliterated, you are completely aware of the God-Self.

The Word *God*

Often we will hear someone say, "I don't like the word *God.*" In fact, sometimes this is said with great vehemence, and we wonder why the speaker should feel so keenly about this word. Requests have come in asking that the word *God* be omitted and some other word substituted, such as *Mind* or *Principle* or perhaps *Reality.* In fact, it is surprising how many different words are preferred to the word *God* when referring to the All.

It is understandable that those who have been rigidly held to a false concept of God during their Sunday school experience should object to this word. It is also understandable that one would not care for this word *God* if it had no definite meaning for him. It is natural to prefer a name to denote God that has genuine meaning to the individual. However, to choose one synonym for God to the exclusion of all others may very well engender a limited concept of the Entirety which is God.

Let us consider some of the synonyms that are preferred to the word *God* and see what they mean, and why they are important to the complete realization of the Allness which is God. Let us begin with the synonym *Mind.*

Now, Mind *is* God, and God could not be the All if God were not Mind. Of course, you know that we are not speaking in metaphysical terminology when we refer to Mind. We are not referring to Mind and Its ideas. We have seen much farther than that. But we are considering Intelligence, for Mind *is* Intelligence. Furthermore, Mind is universal Intelligence, and It is intelligent universally. This means that Intelligence is equally intelligent infinitely and eternally. As we have so often stated, *this is an intelligent Universe*. Indeed It is, and Intelligence *is* this Universe.

Now, we would not say that Consciousness, Life, or Love was excluded from this Universe. Neither would we say that Mind left off at some imaginary point and Consciousness, Life, or Love began at this point. In fact, we would not say that Consciousness, Life, or Love was separable from Intelligence. Most important of all, we would not consider Consciousness to be any more or any less essential to universal Completeness than we know Intelligence to be. Neither would we consider Life or Love to be any more or any less important and necessary than are Consciousness and Mind. It is true that at some given moment we may seem to be more aware of Love than we are of Life, but this does not mean that we consider Life to be any less important than is Love.

The foregoing would be true no matter what synonym we were to choose in the place of the word *God*. To use any synonym for this wonderful word, *God*, can make it appear that God is more or less important or complete as one aspect of Itself. God cannot be qualified in *any* way. God cannot be more God as Mind than God is God as Life or Consciousness or Love. God is equally God as All that God *is*.

Certain it is that God is Reality, but is there an existence that is unreality? When we have said *God*, haven't we said *Reality*? When we have said *God*, haven't we really said *Intelligence* and *Consciousness* and *Love*? Indeed, we have said all of these aspects of God, but we have said much, much more. When we have said *God*, we have said *Everything*, for God *is* Everything. Strictly speaking, every noun in English, or any other language, should be capitalized, for God is Everything that could be designated as a noun.

Please do not mistake the purpose of this article. It is not that anyone can tell you or wishes to tell you what name you should prefer in speaking of God. Rather, it is to present all that is meant when any synonym for God is used. Furthermore, it is being written that you might perhaps experience a greater awareness of the indivisible Entirety which is God. So no matter what synonym you may use in speaking of God, it will be well for you to consciously realize that God is All, All is God. God is Everything, Everything is God.

I love the word *God.* I love to say it. I love to write it, and I love to hear it. I am fully aware that no word can describe God. I also know that all the words in the English language could not describe the Indescribable. Yet I am intensely aware of the fact that this one word says all that can be said about the indescribable, unexplainable, Allness which I call God.

Throughout the ages, there have been those who have tried to explain God, and they have failed. There have been many sincere ones who have even tried to describe God, but they too have found this to be impossible. It is related that many enlightened ones refused to answer when they were queried as to the nature of God. It has been said again and again that the question "What is God?" was generally met with a strict silence.

Words are wonderful instruments, but they can be very tricky and unsatisfying too. Actually, each one of us has to be his own semanticist. Now, this is true because you are the one who knows what any specific word means to you. No attempt to explain or to describe God can be satisfactory because no word or group of words can mean *Everything* to anyone. One who attempts to explain God always faces this disadvantage. However, our way does not seem as yet to be the way of complete silence. So we make use of the instruments—words—which mean God to us, knowing that they are, at best, unsatisfying and incomplete.

One who walks as an illumined Being *knows* God. One who sees the Light knows that he is seeing God, but he also knows that he cannot explain in words That which he sees. Furthermore, he knows that he is not seeing in the ordinary interpretation of the term. He is aware that his Vision is entirely spiritual, and above all, it is universal. It is also true that he is aware of the fact that he *is* the very Essence he sees.

This experience no one can describe or explain. However, I can tell you that the word *God* is most precious, and this is particularly true with those of us who are considered to be of the Western world. It is true that those of the Buddhist faith have other words that mean just what God means to us. But here again, to the Identity, the inner meaning of the word is all that is important.

Perhaps we should not be unduly concerned with the name we use in our contemplation of the universal All. The Bible makes it very clear that God has identified Himself, or Itself, by the name I AM:

> And Moses said unto God, Behold, when I come unto the children of Israel, and shall say unto them, The God of your fathers hath sent me unto you, and they shall say to me, What is his name? what shall I say unto them? And God said unto Moses, I AM THAT I AM: and he said, Thus shalt thou say unto the children of Israel, I AM hath sent me unto you (Exod. 3:13-14).

Yes, I AM is the name by which God may be most clearly perceived. I AM is the name by which God introduces Itself, announces Its presence. But "I am" is also our way of introducing ourselves or announcing our presence. For instance, we will announce our identity by saying, "I am John Jones" or, "I am Mary Smith." If we wish to announce our presence, we will say, "I am here." For this reason, we must be very careful indeed when we speak of God as I AM.

No assumptive human being can say "I am God." As we have often said, *only God can say, "I am God."* When Consciousness is illumined and there is no fallacious sense of being a person, we may find ourselves joyously saying, "I am God" or, "I am that I AM." But Illumined Consciousness really is God being conscious. Thus, as illumined Consciousness, it is God who says, "I am God" and not an assumptive little "I" egotistically attempting to glorify itself.

There has been much misunderstanding, or insufficient understanding, pertaining to these two verses from Exodus. It has been generally believed that God is supposed to have spoken to Moses, but this is impossible. For if this could be, God would have to be God and Moses would have to be someone separate from, or other than, God. So we must ask ourselves *who was saying* I AM THAT I AM and *to whom were these words being spoken*?

It is obvious that Moses was illumined during this experience. In illumination we *know* that God is the Entirety of our Being. We actually know and experience *being* the universal All which *is* God. That which is true of us in illumination was also true of Moses when he was illumined. So Moses must have known that there was no God outside of, or other than, his own Identity who was talking to him.

In illumination there is such complete awareness of being the One alone that it would be impossible for us to imagine a voice that was other than the Voice of our own Consciousness. Thus, Moses must have known that he was hearing his own words and that the Voice he heard was *his* Voice. This is true because Moses was the speaker and the hearer. He was the One who spoke and the One who heard the words.

Incidentally, those of you who have attended classes in the Ultimate know that we have had this same exact experience. This has been particularly true during our seminars. We have been intensely aware that the speaker and the hearer were the same One. We have also known that the words being spoken were present in and as the Consciousness of the One who heard the words. In this way, we can understand how it was, and why it was, that Moses was really speaking and hearing the Voice of his own Consciousness.

The words I AM THAT are of tremendous importance. No one can say, "I am God" unless he can—with understanding—say, "I am That." You see, in illumination we are aware of *being* all that we see. No matter what we see, whether it be trees, flowers, planets, suns, or whatever, we realize that *we are That*. We are aware that we are inseparable from all we see. We are not aware of dividing lines or of anything partial. Rather, we are aware of *being* the infinite, indivisible Essence and Its activity.

In other words, we are aware that all we are seeing is our own Consciousness, and this Consciousness is the Essence of all Form as well as the Form of all Essence. This Consciousness, which is *our* Consciousness, is the activity of the infinite Essence, and this activity is our own Consciousness in action. This, dear One, explains how it is, and why it is, that we can say, "I am That" when we are illumined. This also explains why we cannot say, "I am That" or, "I am God" unless we are consciously illumined.

An illumined experience is a God-experience. It is God experiencing *being* Itself. You are the one who has the experience, so you are the one who is experiencing *being* your Self. It is in this glorious experience that you really *know* God, and you know God to be your Self. It is also in this same experience that you are really your Self, and you know your Self to be That which you have called

God. It is in this experience that you know there are no words with which to describe that which you have discovered your Self to be. If you were to speak, you could only say, "I am" or perhaps, "I am That."

You see, your *only* awareness is a consciousness of being, of existing. So naturally, all that you could say would be, "I am." This is why it is impossible to find any word in English or any other language which really means God. This also explains why it is impossible for any synonym to be sufficient when speaking of God. However, the word *God* of Itself is not a synonym *for* God. For this reason, it is the only word I know that means *Everything*.

As a rule, we cannot use the words I AM or I AM THAT in our daily conversation. But we can say *God*, knowing that we have said Everything. We have said all the *Essence*, all the *Intelligence*, all the *Life*, all the *Consciousness*, and all the *Love* there is. And we have also said much more than this. We have said more than any or all nouns could say. Furthermore, we have said *Omniaction*, or all the Activity there is and all that acts. Oh, it is wonderful what you can realize when you say this little three-letter word, *God*.

My Burden Is Light

Jesus is often depicted as a "man of sorrows," and he is pictured as being bowed down by the burden of his responsibility for a sinning, suffering world. Yet Jesus did not accept this picture as exemplifying himself. As evidence of this fact, he said:

> Come unto me, all ye that labour and are heavy laden, and I will give you rest (Matt. 11:28).

Jesus was not burdened, but he knew that others seemed to be laboring under the false burden of illusory materiality.

When Jesus said, "Come unto me," he certainly did not mean that he was inviting others to come to him as a personal savior. Rather, he was inviting them to come into a realization of their Christhood, and he knew that *only* in this way could they discover themselves to be free from labor, weariness, or bondage of *any* nature. The "I" that was to give them rest was the *I* of their own Consciousness.

> Take my yoke upon you and learn of me, for I am meek and lowly in heart: and ye shall find rest unto your soul; For my yoke is easy, and my burden is light (Matt. 11:29-30).

Here Jesus is asking them to accept his Christ-Identity as their own Identity. He was also revealing that the greatest true humility was essential if they were to realize themselves to be the Christ-Identity. He knew that to imagine the assumptive human self to be the God-Self was to be deluded indeed, and he knew that this illusion was fraught with sorrow, burden, and bondage. Whenever an assumptive little "I" tries to do something or to be something of itself, it is falsely *assuming* that it is the Intelligence, it is the Consciousness, it is the power that is God alone. We know that assumptive, self-important man would vehemently deny that this is true. Nonetheless, it *is* true. It is just that the illusion called man is not aware of what he is really assuming when he tries to be something of himself.

The Christ-Consciousness is "meek and lowly in heart." It is fully aware of the utter futility of attempting to do something or to be something of Itself, something which could be other than God. However, this same Christ-Consciousness is not an awareness of false humility. It is not self-debasing, and It never encourages injustice or imposition. The Christ-Consciousness is true humility because It knows that only because God *is* can It be. This is why this Consciousness does not try to be something of Itself.

It is in this true humility that the seeming burdens drop away, and that which *seemed* to be bondage is known to be utterly without existence. You will note that Jesus said, "And ye shall find rest unto your souls." Obviously, Jesus was not offering to provide rest for the people. Rather, he was saying, in effect, "You are to discover your own rest, and you will discover it when you realize that your Soul is your Christ-Consciousness."

It is wonderful to realize the Absolute Truths revealed in just these three verses from Matthew, and it is paradoxical that these Truths seem to have been hidden by a veil of materialistic misunderstanding. However, we can rejoice that we do perceive the genuine significance which they express.

Now let us perceive just how our perception of this significance pertains to our daily affairs. One of the most deceptive of all illusions is a false sense of responsibility. It is this illusion that keeps us trying to do something *for* someone or *about* some situation. You see, it is always the illusory that imagines it must *do* something for itself or for one whom it calls another. So long as one imagines himself to be something of himself, he is going to *do* something of himself, and it is in this attempt to do something of himself that the burdens, the weariness, and the frustrations seemingly occur. So the false sense of responsibility is never obliterated until it is fully realized that no one exists of himself who can do anything.

No one is responsible for one whom he calls "another." In fact, we are not responsible for ourselves. As an example, can we say that we are responsible for the fact that we exist? No, of course not. Then how is it that we can be responsible for ourselves? We can't, and actually we know this to be true. But it is also true that we are not responsible for the fact that the one we call "another" exists.

Of course, we are not speaking of illusory beings called humans. We are speaking of the genuine and *only* Identity of all of us. Only if there were such a thing as birth could there actually be a responsibility for the existence of another, and *there is no birth.* Only if we could bring ourselves into being could we be responsible for ourselves. We never began, so how could we have been brought into existence? How could we have brought ourselves into existence? We couldn't and we didn't. Thus, we are not burdened with responsibility.

It is amazing how this false sense of responsibility will seem to creep into our Consciousness. For instance, we are compassionate, and this is as it should be. Love is *always* compassionate. But we seem to feel that our compassion impels us to *do* something for or about someone or something. This is particularly noticeable with those of us who are helping others. If we are not vigilant, the little "I" will seem to creep in as a false sense of responsibility for the one who seems to need help. Then we apparently become concerned and feel that we are doing something of ourselves.

By this same token, if the evidence of perfection is not immediate, we tend to limit, or worse, condemn ourselves. This is so subtle because in our very effort to do something for someone or something, we have accepted their seeming problem. If it seems to be our responsibility, then it is also going to appear to be our problem. This being true, we find ourselves in the position of trying to rid another of something which we are claiming and hugging to ourselves. As an example of this fact, those who are called practitioners have actually seemed to take on the evidence of that which they were trying to heal for someone else. Let us not be deluded in this way.

Let us be very clear on this point: we do not ignore a plea for help. Neither do we close our eyes to another's seeming need, whether or not this one has asked for help. But we don't try to do something, of ourselves, about It. Once we are aware of that which *seems* to be the problem, we are not concerned about the *seeming*. Least of all do we try to do something about it. We know that there is no problem and that *there is no one having a problem*. Thus, we are not responsible for healing or removing the illusory problem, and neither are we responsible for the illusory concept called man who seems to have a problem.

But we are concerned with something. We are concerned with *what we know to be true*. This is an *active* concern. We don't dawdle; we are intensely active. But our activity is not one of *doing something for someone*; neither is it the activity of *doing something about some problem*. It is all a matter of Consciousness. Our concern is entirely in the realm of Consciousness. (What other realm is there?)

The Consciousness we *are* is actively perceiving the Truth. No matter what the seeming problem, we are consciously active in our perception of *that which is true* instead of that which *seems* to be true. If death seems to be imminent, we are intensely aware that eternal, omnipresent, irresistible, irrepressible Life is the *only* Life that is alive. If sadness or grief seems to be apparent, we are conscious of the universal, uninterrupted Joy which is all that can exist or be known. If there seems to be lack, we actively perceive the omnipresence of Completeness. We are aware that God, the Universe, is complete as every aspect of Itself. If deterioration or age seems to present itself, we are conscious of the fact that eternal, immutable Life is the *only* Life that is alive or that can be alive.

The foregoing gives just a brief example of what our "busy-ness" is when called upon for help. It is apparent that we do not feel responsible for a problem that does not exist. Neither do we accept responsibility for the welfare and perfection of one who never had or experienced a nonexistent problem.

Jesus knew that others seemed to be burdened by numerous problems. He was compassionate. He did not turn away from them, but Jesus did not accept responsibility. He was immune. He knew that the only loving way to act was to be *actively* conscious of the Truth of any situation. He also knew that the only way anyone could be completely free of all illusory burdens was to know what constituted his Identity, his Being, and his Body.

Jesus was completely free of the little assumptive "I." This is why he was immune to any false sense of responsibility. Our necessity is absolute freedom from any fallacious sense of being a person. It means the complete freedom from all burdens and freedom from bondage. To the extent that the little "I" appears to be active, the activity of the *I* that I am appears to fluctuate. And it is the infinite *I* that evidences Its activity as the evidence of complete perfection, freedom, and abundance.

To be free from the fallacious, little personal sense of being means to be free from all dualism, and of course, dualism is the basic illusion. Indeed, the burden *is* light when we no longer seem to carry a seeming weight of dualistic illusion. But most glorious of all is the fact that we see and experience the *evidence* of our freedom as the evidence of the freedom of the one we call another. So we have dispensed with the illusion of false responsibility.

Now let us see and experience the eternal, uninterrupted Perfection which has always been and will ever be all that is here. Thus, we will see and experience the evidence of this Perfection as our own Entirety, and we will see it as the Entirety which we call others.

Questions and Answers

Q: Should students of the Ultimate engage in political activity?

A: I suppose Jesus would answer this question by saying, "Render to Caesar the things that are Caesar's, and to God the things that are God's" (Mark 12:17).

Thus do we also render unto Caesar the things that are Caesar's, and to God the things that are God's. However, this does not mean it is necessary for us to become embroiled in the actual mechanics of political machinery. Of course, each one of us must decide for himself about this—and every other matter.

I have felt that it was right to vote, and generally I have done so. But I do not depend upon any political demagoguery to inform me as to how to vote. In fact, I do not listen to political speeches, and neither do I read them. As in everything else, I depend entirely upon Mind, which is the Intelligence of everyone, in order to act intelligently.

In the illusory sense of government by men, it does seem necessary to have politics and politicians. It also seems necessary to have political organizations. Those who feel it incumbent upon them to be active politically should continue in this activity so long as they feel it's right for them. In fact, it would be helpful if all political workers were students of the Absolute. But let us frequently remind ourselves that there is *One* who governs, and this One is God—infinite Love, Principle, Intelligence. We do not place our faith in "man with breath in his nostrils" because we know that he is not the genuine and only Identity, which is God identified. Actually, each one of us is his own governor and his own government. This is true because each Identity is God identified, and God is the One who governs. Furthermore, God governs Itself only.

Students of the Ultimate are good citizens. We live normally, and we act intelligently. Above all, we act lovingly, and this is inevitable—for we *are* Love Itself. Thus, we are just, honest, and ethical. But we do not depend upon so-called human government for our freedom, for our supply, or for our protection. We act in the way that appears right at the moment, in the same way that Jesus permitted himself to be baptized. We suffer it to be so now because this is the way that seems right now. But we do not really descend to the illusion that we are mortals dependent upon or subject to the assumptive laws made by assumptive man. Nonetheless, we are law-abiding *by choice* and not by necessity.

Humility

Oh, great and true humility,
Revealing the futility
Of human ego, pride,
In this I must abide.
May I forever realize
That falsity can ne'er disguise
The undivided One
Beside whom there is none
To do, to think, to have, or be,
No one to hear, and none to see.
Not even can the Son
Be other than the One,
E'en though Identity is true,
The One identified as You,
Must be the All, Infinity,
Revealed as your divinity.

Light and Love,
Marie S. Watts

June 1963

In the beginning was the Word, and the Word was with God, and the Word was God.

—John 1:1

Dear One,

No doubt you have received your notice of the coming seminar. Already new and glorious revelations are being experienced, as I contemplate this illuminating event. Some of you have signified your intention of being with us, and our Heart rejoices. Many of you will be arriving from what the world would call great distances. Yet isn't it wonderful to know that there is no distance? If there is no space, and there isn't, there can be no distance. This fact is becoming increasingly apparent in and as my Consciousness. I note that so-called miles are traversed with no sense of having traveled at all.

A wonderfully enlightened student, who lives in New York, had this experience. She drove to Atlanta to attend the class. On the drive back, after the class, she drove over five hundred miles in one day, and she had no awareness of traveling, of weariness or strain, or even of doing anything of herself. This was an entirely new experience for her, as she had always before seemed to be very aware of miles traveled and to experience fatigue. What takes place is wonderful when the Consciousness is enlightened—illumined—and we *know* what we are and *why* we are what we are.

More and more we are realizing that we can be anywhere without having to travel in order to be aware of being where we are. As the illusion of time and space disperses, we are conscious of the fact that there can be no "there" because no matter where we are, it is "here" to us at the moment.

One day, the indivisible, infinite nature of all Consciousness will be realized so completely that travel as it is now known will be unknown. There is a dawning recognition of this fact, even among our spacemen. This is most encouraging.

It is impossible to close without thanking you again for your many letters expressing such great joy and appreciation for the writings of the Ultimate. Please know that I am just as grateful for these revelations as you are, and your letters do enhance my joy in this activity. While I know that this Truth *is* true, it is gratifying to hear and see abundant evidence of its Truth.

Being the Light

If we were to accept the daily news reports as fact, we would certainly feel that the world, including our own nation, was in dire straits. Certain it is that the *appearance* of the world situation is disturbing. But the Bible makes a very definite statement about judging that which *appears* to be, but *is not*, genuine:

> Judge not according to the appearance, but judge righteous judgment (John 7:24).

To judge righteous judgment means to judge rightly, to perceive that which is right and true instead of accepting as genuine an appearance of something that is not true.

God *is* All. Every Truth we know must stem from this one basic fact. If God be All, then this world is God in Essence and in Activity. If this is not true, then either God is not All, or else there is no such thing as this world, as it *appears* to be. We have seen irrefutable proof, again and again, that God is All. So this fact must stand as proven.

But there can be no doubt that there *is* something here, which we call the world. God being All, this Something which is here cannot be what it *appears* to be because God is Peace, Love, perfect Harmony, and Joy. So it is necessary for us to perceive just what constitutes this world and why it has to be what it genuinely *is*.

We cannot deny that there is Something existing which we call the world. It is futile to deny that this world consists of an infinite variety of aspects and that these aspects comprise its Completeness. The seeming difficulty of the world today is due to the illusion that the Something which comprises the world is *divided* into aspects. *In any illusion of inharmony, there is always the fallacious acceptance of division.* An entire book could be written on the fallacy of separateness. However, just now, let us pursue the basic facts that are essential for us to realize at the moment.

We can consider the oceans of the world as an aspect of its Completeness. We can also perceive that continents, mountains, plains, deserts, forests, etc., are aspects of the Completeness which we call the world. It is not too difficult to realize that the continents, oceans, mountains, plains, etc., do not separate the world into little worlds.

The seeming difficulty arises when we consider that which is called the mind of man. Ah, right here is where the false sense of separation enters the picture. Therefore, the seeming division of the world is not a division of the world itself. Rather, it is the assumptive mind of "man with breath in his nostrils" which apparently attempts to divide the one world into separate little worlds of his own. So if we are to see through this apparent division of the world, we must first see through that fallacy called the mind of man.

The assumptive mind of man is presumed to become a separate mind at that first illusion—birth. Thus, the supposed event called birth is the first and basic delusion of separateness. All other misconceptions of division or separation stem from this first illusion. But we know that Mind, or Intelligence, is not born. God is the *only* Mind, and the Mind which is eternal Intelligence cannot begin or be born. So our necessity is to realize that the genuine and only Mind in existence is that beginningless, endless Mind that has no awareness of division or separation. It is comparatively easy to proceed from this realization to the perception that Life, Consciousness, and Love are as inseparable as is Intelligence. Once we are fully aware of this fact, the true nature of the world in all its aspects is vividly apparent.

As stated before, continents, oceans, mountains are distinct aspects of the Completeness which constitutes the world. Trees, flowers, animals, birds, etc., are also distinct aspects of that which we call the world. Right here it would be well to realize that our world, or Earth Planet, is but one aspect of the Infinite All, which is God, or the Universe.

However, at the moment, let us continue with our exploration of the Earth Planet, which we call the world. The oceans are not opposing or threatening one another. The lands, called continents, are not attempting to possess each other. It is only the little assumptive mind of man that seems to oppose, threaten, attempt to enslave, or to possess other lands and peoples. It is this same assumptive born mind that attempts to possess and enslave through chicanery, dishonesty, brutality, and destructive activities. Of course, war is the zenith of the destructive efforts of the illusory born mind's attempt to inflate itself.

Now, these *apparent* illusions of a supposedly born mind are certainly not very pleasant to read about. Neither is it necessary to dwell upon them any further. It was necessary to point out certain idiosyncrasies of the assumptive mind of man in order to clarify the genuine, perfect world in all its aspects. The important fact to recognize is that the fallacious appearance of division must be recognized and expelled if we are to fulfill our purpose in the affairs of the world today.

We cannot ignore the false evidence which is apparently so widely accepted to be true. The Truth we *know* must fulfill Its purpose in our affairs, and particularly in the affairs of this apparently troubled world. So let us perceive the way our perception of Truth can be a tremendous power in world affairs.

It is well to realize that the affairs of the world are *our* affairs. We are not isolated beings with selfish, little personal lives. Rather, we are aware of being the very Presence of the omniactive Mind which does reveal Itself as Intelligence, Life, Consciousness, Love.

Of course, the first necessity for us is to realize the indivisible nature of our Consciousness. It would be well to remind ourselves of the wonderful proof of this fact, which takes place during our seminars. Briefly, let us recall our experiences during these momentous events, and that our revelations are experienced by many who are supposedly thousands of miles away. We know this seeming miracle to be an actual experience, and we have ample proof of this fact. We also know that the only answer to this seeming miracle lies in the fact that Consciousness is inseparable. This is the secret of how it is possible for each one of us to be an active power in this seemingly troubled world.

We do not practice mental telepathy. We do not send out thoughts. We do nothing that can be termed human thinking, meditation, or concentration. Rather, we are aware of the infinite, indivisible Nature of every Truth we are realizing and the inseparable Nature of the Consciousness which is aware of any Truth.

We are also aware of the fact that there is neither time nor space which can act as an obstruction to our revelations.

We know there are no barriers in or as Consciousness, and we know that there are no lines of demarcation which can separate Consciousness into consciousnesses. With this realization, let us proceed to perceive just what *is* necessary to realize when our Consciousness is actively focused upon the affairs of the world.

First, last, and always, *God is All, All is God.* Love, Intelligence, Life, Consciousness constitute the Allness which is God. Thus, loving, living, conscious Intelligence is the *only* Mind in existence. This omnipresent Mind, which is Love, exists in Its fullness, Its completeness, right here and now. It exists as the *only* Intelligence that is, or can be, functioning in and as this world and its affairs. This Mind is as omnipresent and as impersonal as is the air or the sunlight.

We know there is a tremendous spiritual awakening going on in the world today. There is evidence of this fact on every side. We have no way to know how much our awareness of the indivisible nature of Consciousness may have helped, and may be helping, in this awakening. Of course, although it *seems* to be an awakening, the word *awakening* is not quite the right word to express what is taking place. Perhaps a better way to say it would be that the one infinite, conscious, living Intelligence is insisting upon revealing Itself to be *the only Presence and the only Power*. In any event, we do know that the world Consciousness seems to be more open and receptive during the last while.

We know that our awareness of the Presence of omnipotent, loving, intelligent Consciousness is unconfined. Every Truth we know to be true is known everywhere and *equally* everywhere. Thus, wherever Consciousness is open and receptive to any Truth, the Truth we are contemplating must be revealed. So whenever that great revelation of omnipresent Love is experienced as our Consciousness, we can know that It is also present and revealed *in and as the Consciousness of everyone in the world.* When we realize that *we are that perfect Love in which there is no fear*, we can realize also that our revelation of this fact is being experienced by all who are conscious of existing.

No matter how evil, dishonest, brutal, or scheming a so-called leader may *seem* to be, we know that the only Consciousness is the Intelligence which is principled, loving, just, and peaceful. A warring consciousness is impossible. A mind that desires to rob and enslave others is not intelligent because *only Intelligence is intelligent*. Therefore, the non-mind that seems to operate as another intelligence is not capable of scheming or carrying out its seemingly evil schemes. Being actually without intelligence, it is without existence, for Intelligence is omnipresent. It is illusion dispersing itself, and it cannot hurt or harm the living, loving, conscious Intelligence which is God. This Intelligence is intelligent as You, as Me, and as Everyone in existence.

We know what constitutes substance. We know that the Body is indestructible and that there is no substance that can destroy Consciousness, Intelligence, Life, Love. So we know that the Body cannot be destroyed because conscious, living, loving Intelligence *constitutes* the indestructible Body of Light. The Body of Light is our *only* Body, and even if there were a destructive element called nuclear warfare, it would be incapable of destroying the Body of Light. *It is essential, though, to realize that there is no destructive substance or power*. We do not make affirmations and denials about this matter. We simply know that a destructive element is an impossibility because God is the only Substance, the only Life, and the only Activity. God *is* this world, and God is *all* that exists as this world and everyone who inhabits it.

Because we realize the indivisible Nature of our Consciousness, we should be actively perceiving the Truth in and *as* the affairs of the world. Whenever we are in contemplation, it would be well to realize that every Truth we are contemplating is being revealed within and as the Consciousness of innumerable ones throughout the world. In all our contemplation, let us realize the indivisible infinity of the Consciousness which perceives whatever Truth we are perceiving. Let us realize that the Love we are experiencing is being *consciously* experienced throughout the entire world. Let us perceive that the peace we are experiencing is being consciously experienced as everyone who is conscious. Let us realize that the Life which is alive as our Life is alive *as indestructible Life* everywhere, in and as this living world.

Above all, let us be aware of the infinite power of our awareness of this Truth, and let us realize that our awareness of this Truth is the *only Power*. It is, you know, because *only* the Mind which is God can be aware of any Truth. Thus, the Consciousness that you are and that I am *is* omnipotent, loving, living, conscious Mind, aware of *being* what It is and All that It is.

It is unnecessary to tell us that *no little egotistical, nonexistent human mind can know the Truth or make these claims.* It is not even possible to contemplate these glorious Truths so long as there is any illusion of a personal ego *seeming* to be around. But oh, when all so-called human desire, ambition, false sense of self is dispelled, then and *only* then does God reveal His glorious Self to be the *only* Self of you, of me, and of all.

All of you are aware of the necessity to recognize your complete nothingness as a personal self. You also know just how to obliterate this fallacious illusion. But it is well to frequently renew our awareness that *of ourselves we are nothing, can be nothing, have nothing, do nothing*. We must be very careful indeed that the illusory little ego does not attempt to parade around under the guise of the *only* One who can know Itself to be anything.

We should be particularly alert to this temptation right now because the works of the Ultimate are becoming so well known. We must be careful that we do not claim for ourselves any Truth that we do not claim to be true world-wide and universally. If we steadily continue to recognize that only because God *is* can we be, our humility will ensure ever greater revelations. So let us continue to know that *to God belongs the glory*, and God is the *only* One who can be glorified.

Prayer Is Power

If I were to pray in the old orthodox way, my prayer would always be, "Oh, God, let there be no Marie."

When we were children, we prayed as children, and often our prayers were answered. Yet more often our prayers remained unanswered, and we wondered just why this should be. We know that the prayers of those who are still children are often answered. There is irrefutable proof of this fact.

Increasingly the orthodox churches are including healing in their ministry, and increasingly they are experiencing answers to their prayers for healing. We rejoice in this proof of the Presence of God right here and now. This is particularly important right now because there seems to be an organized denial that there *is* a God. In the proven answers to the prayers of those of orthodox faith, this denial of God is obviously refuted.

This refutation is of vital importance to the world today and to us. Let us never feel superior to the sincere prayers of simple faith. Rather, let us be glad that these prayers are sometimes answered and that the answers are proof to the world that *there is a God*. Furthermore, herein is proof to the world that God is present and that God *is* Power.

Of course, we cannot return to orthodoxy, but we can, and should, recognize that which is good in all faiths. We should also understand how it is, and why it is, that sometimes the prayers of simple faith are answered. There are certain aspects present in every prayer of simple faith when the prayer is answered by that which is called healing. Let us perceive what these aspects in common are and why the so-called healing is evidenced.

Of course, we must dismiss those pseudo cases of healing, where emotionalism acts as a mesmeric spell and often the one who *seems* to be healed will ultimately discover that there was no healing. Furthermore, such a one may seem to be worse than ever before. We are not considering the seeming charlatans in the healing ministry. But we are discussing the prayers of sincerity, those prayers in which what is called healing seems to take place.

Whenever a prayer of sincerity is answered and Perfection is manifested, there is, at least for the moment, an *unselfed* appeal to God. The one who prays may feel that the disease is real and that he is in great need of healing. But for the moment, he has admitted his utter inability to do anything "of himself" about this so-called condition.

He probably does not realize this to be true, but the very basic principle of the Allness of God is revealed in this moment of utter human helplessness. In this moment, God alone is important in his Consciousness, and this complete obliteration of the little suffering self reveals the God who was already present *as* his only Consciousness. Whether one prays for himself or someone of sincerity prays for him, the Principle remains the same. The prayer is a *complete obliteration of the little personal self* in either the one who prays or the one for whom the prayer is uttered.

Furthermore, the prayer is a humble admission that of himself so-called man can do nothing.

These are the two basic principles of the answers to the prayers of simple faith. Back of these two principles is the vitally important fact that God *is* All and All *is* God. Sometimes it seems paradoxical that God, the All, insists upon revealing Itself not because of our efforts but despite them.

We are not children. We have obeyed the injunction in Proverbs:

> Wisdom is the principle thing, therefore get wisdom: and with all thy getting, get understanding (Prov. 4:7).

These are words of wisdom, but Solomon has words of even greater wisdom:

> Trust in the Lord with all thine heart, and lean not unto thine own understanding (Prov. 3:5).

Ah, here is where we should be very alert. We should be very sure that we are not depending upon any so-called human understanding for the solutions to seeming problems. The assumptive human mind cannot even know God, so how could it possibly have wisdom and an understanding of God?

Most of us have studied, read, pondered, and earnestly sought to acquire wisdom. We have followed many and diverse paths in our search. Each path fulfilled a definite aspect of our seeming search. We were "getting wisdom." We were becoming more aware of the basic Principles which constitute God, the Universe, and our own Identities.

But the wisdom of itself was not enough. We arrived at the point where it did not satisfy; neither did it always enable us to see through all of our seeming problems. So we continued on, until we arrived at the *Heart* of the entire understanding which wisdom had helped to reveal.

The Heart of all understanding is the basic fact: *God is All; thus, All is God.* Therefore, that which is called man is nonexistent as an independent entity or identity. Man, with breath in his nostrils, does not exist. This fact reveals that even that which seemed to be our search was announcing, and being God. We cannot take any credit, even for that which we have considered to be *our* search. Neither can we condemn those who do not seem to be interested in searching. The realization that God *is* All includes the perception that God is *eternally* All. Thus, that which seemed to be a search for God *was* God, being All, and revealing Its Allness.

A prayer of an understanding Heart is power. This prayer is never a prayer of supplication. It is never directed *to* God. It is not a matter of mental gymnastics—of methods, formulas, etc. Neither is it a matter of affirmations and denials. It is not a matter of doing or thinking, either. All of these methods have to do with the assumptive "man with breath in his nostrils." But this is not the prayer of the understanding Heart.

Prayer *is* power when the fact is realized that God is the Power. This realization precludes the possibility of another power called a reasoning, thinking, human mind. It completely cancels any illusion that a human mind exists or that it can do anything, have anything, or be anything. It is in this obliteration of the fallacious human mind that the *only* Mind, which is God, reveals what God knows to be true.

Prayer is power when it is realized that God is the only Presence, *the only One present.* In this realization, the assumptive mind of man does not exist. Therefore, the one and only Mind which is God is apparent. In this way, that which God knows to be true is revealed and evidenced. So the first requisite for the prayer of understanding is the complete obliteration of the illusory personal self. This means that we are to realize that of ourselves we can know nothing, do nothing, have nothing, be nothing. It means that we perceive the utter futility of any assumptive, puny effort to change or to heal anything.

It is not until we realize that we of ourselves are nothing that we can even know the true meaning of prayer. In this completely unselfed realization, we discover that our prayer is already answered. Thus, we shall perceive how it is, and why it is, that the illumined one could joyously say:

> And it shall come to pass, that before they call, I will answer; and while they are yet speaking, I will hear (Isa. 65:24).

Questions and Answers

Q: Why do you avoid the expression "Mind and its idea"?

A: In that which I shall call "my search" for God, I came to Christian Science. It was at this point that I first encountered the expression "Mind and its idea." I believe that Mary Baker Eddy was the first one to use this expression, and it served a wonderful purpose for me. It revealed the possibility that God could be in me and that I could be in God. It clarified how this could be the case.

I do not use this expression now because it has served its purpose in my experience. I find that it no longer satisfies. I prefer the expression *Consciousness identified.* This latter expression more clearly states the instantaneousness of the Oneness which is God, identified as You, as Me, and as All. There can be no illusion of time or space intervening between Consciousness and Its identification of *Itself.* There could be a connotation of time *before* an idea appeared in Mind. Ideas can seem to come and to go. The

Identity, which is Consciousness identified, must be as eternal as is the Consciousness which identifies Itself.

Abundance

Oh, who am I that I should yearn
For health or wealth or things?
Do I not know that I must turn
And see that even kings
Are poor indeed, if they know not
That God alone is All,
And earthly kingdoms come to naught,
For all but God must fall.

Illusion's man must disappear
In order that His Light
Obliterate all yearning, fear,
All lack, all trouble, blight;
His Presence is fore'er complete
As Health and Wealth are shown
To be His Allness, now replete,
He is the One, alone.

Light and Love,
Marie S. Watts

July 1963

In the beginning was the Word, and the Word was with God, and the Word was God.

—John 1:1

Dear One,

The words *thank you* are such puny instruments through which to express my great thanks to you. Your letters act as a constant wellspring of Joy to my daily experience. Every day I am more aware of the fact that this is our activity. Every day your letters report that you are experiencing being your own revelator and your own revelation. Thus does God, who is all there is of your Identity and mine, fulfill Its purpose as this Activity.

We know so well that we are not instruments, or channels, through which this God-activity flows. We know that in order to be an instrument or a channel for God, we would have to be something or someone separate from, or other than, God. We know so well that God being All, a channel through which God flowed would be entirely impossible. Oh, how glorious is the revelation that God—the All—is *equally present* throughout Infinity and Eternity. This means there is nothing extraneous to God and there is no absence of God.

Your Boundless Consciousness

There is one aspect of Existence which seems to be very puzzling to students of Truth. This is the fact that each Identity is infinite, boundless, immeasurable. Often the student will, unwittingly, avoid the acceptance of this Truth. Yet the full and complete recognition and acceptance of our infinitude is of paramount importance for each one of us. We tend to omit the contemplation of our boundless Identity because it appears to be unbelievable, or at least unreasonable. Then too, until our infinity is realized, it seems the very height of egotism and selfishness to accept it.

There is an aspect of illumination in which the spaceless, timeless Universe is perceived. In this illumination, the illumined one is cognizant of the fact that he or she is boundless. Furthermore, this aspect of illumination reveals irrefutably that the Identity is the infinite, eternal Universe and everything that he perceives. Needless to say, there can be no egotism in this perception. Rather, there is a tremendous humility that is known to be entirely selfless. Although the illumined One is aware of being an Identity, he has no awareness of being a person, and least of all does he perceive himself to be a human, or a mortal, being.

The actual meaning of the word *freedom* can never be known until the Identity recognizes his infinite, eternal, boundless Self. Every seeming boundary, whether it be called a time boundary or a space boundary, must be cancelled if one is to realize and experience complete freedom.

For instance, birth could not be called the beginning of a time boundary as far as an individual is concerned, and death would not be the ending of that boundary. The interim between what is called birth and death would be limited by the time of the beginning and the time of the ending of the life of an assumptive human. So the very first illusion of so-called human life is that of being limited by a time boundary. But the pseudo limitation does not stop with this illusion. It appears to govern every aspect of the life and the experience of so-called human beings.

Even the Bible portrays the lot of the supposedly human being as limited:

> The days of our years are threescore years and ten; and if by reason of strength they be fourscore years, yet is

their strength labour and sorrow; for it is soon cut off, and we fly away (Ps. 90:10).

Unfortunately this gloomy portrayal of the individual has been accepted as the norm, and it is considered to be quite exceptional for one to be a living refutation of this fallacy. All of us are familiar with the further false aspects of limitation imposed upon the individual who is said to be born.

For instance, there is supposedly a limited time in which to be a joyous, carefree child; then there is another time in which the individual must go through an uncertain period of adolescence, and what a trial that is. This period is followed by another limited period of maturity. Then the trouble is really supposed to begin and to continue until the individual's allotted time to live has expired.

Now, of course, these are not pleasant things to speak about, but neither are they pleasant to seem to experience. There are innumerable aspects of the fallacy called time and its boundaries. But for our present purpose, it is more important to explore the illusion of bondage called space.

It does seem simpler to conceive of one's Identity as being eternal than it is to perceive that the Identity is infinite. This disparity stems from the fact that space is a seemingly visible aspect that is visible and measurable by visual means. Furthermore, it appears that space is partitioned into visual blocks or degrees of density. Thus, we are inclined to confine the omnipresent, infinite All within these apparent blocks or partitions. This accounts for our seeming inability to perceive the boundless, limitless, indivisible nature of our Consciousness.

If you gaze into the sky and try to draw an imaginary circle around yourself, you will discover that you cannot even imagine yourself to be *enclosed within* this imagined circle. You cannot say that your Consciousness ends at the point where the so-called human vision ends. For instance, you do not have to humanly see any particular city or area in order to be conscious of that specific city or area. Wherever your Consciousness is focused, *you are*. This is true because your Consciousness *is* you. It is your Identity. Contemplation of this fact will reveal, within and as your Consciousness, your unconfined, immeasurable Self.

Wherever your attention is focused, *there* are you. This does not mean you are projected or have projected yourself to another point in so-called space. It does mean that you are conscious of *being* right where your attention is focused. This would be impossible if your Consciousness were enclosed within a certain area. Yet many of us have discovered that we can consciously be wherever our Consciousness is focused, and there is no such thing as time involved. Rather, our awareness of *being* everywhere, anywhere, is simultaneous with the focusing of our attention.

The assumptive human mind does not enter into this consideration in any way. You do not visualize, you do not try to imagine yourself anywhere. You see, it is in this same fallacious human mind where the belief is that you are confined to this immediate environment. But the genuine and *only* Mind knows Itself to be unconfined. This is *your* Mind, *your* Consciousness, and *your* Identity.

Consciousness is not enclosed. It is not trapped and confined within certain compartments. There is no solidity that can block Consciousness into little blocks of Itself. Consciousness is equally present everywhere and eternally. But as far as you are concerned, your Consciousness is consciously present right where your attention is focused at any given moment. However, this does not mean that your Consciousness is confined where It is focused.

I know that this is a tremendous subject to attempt to clarify in just this one article. Yet the basic Truths of this aspect of your Being have been stated, and this should be helpful to those of you who wish to "tune in" during our seminar.

Of course, we will be realizing this same Truth. We will be aware of the fact that our Consciousness is as unconfined as is your Universal Truth and that It is equally true throughout Infinity and Eternity. We will perceive that there is nothing in existence which can act as a circumference to our conscious awareness of Truth. We shall be intensely aware of the indivisible nature of Consciousness.

Whether this Consciousness is supposed to be your Consciousness or our Consciousness is not important. What is important is the fact that Consciousness is limitless, boundless, immeasurable. Therefore, all seeming boundaries are obliterated, and the one infinite Consciousness will be, and is, revealing Itself as the Consciousness of each one of us.

Contemplate these Truths, dear One, and the glory that is God will reveal Itself to be your *only* Self.

Stand Fast

> Stand fast therefore in the liberty wherewith Christ hath made us free, and be not entangled again with the yoke of bondage (Gal. 5:1).

Paul's exhortation to stand fast is certainly applicable for those of us who are seeing beyond dualism. At the root of all dualism is the illusion that the Identity is something or someone separate from, or other than, God. So long as assumptive man believes that he is separate from God, he is going to accept the fallacy that he is separate from the one he calls "another." But this is not all; this illusion of separation can be traced right through every difficulty we seem to encounter or experience.

What is the meaning of the statement "Christ hath made us free"? To be free from dualism is to be free indeed. To be free from all dualism is to be free from all that appears to be evil. It makes no difference whether trouble should appear to be mental, physical, financial, or whatever—the realization that our very existence is God existing means that we are free.

Needless to say, this realization precludes the possibility of any illusion of dualism. Christ, our God-Identity, has made us free. Christ, our God-Identity, reveals that eternally we are free and never were we in bondage. When the genuine Self is perceived, the Christ is revealed. This is true because the Christ is the actual and *only* Self. To perceive and to experience *being* the Christ is to perceive and experience complete liberty. Liberty is freedom, and freedom means to be free in *all* ways. However, the basic freedom is freedom from dualism.

We would assume that everyone, having once realized his Christ-Self, would never be "entangled again with the yoke of bondage." However, the world of appearance does sometimes seem very real, and it is so easy to again be ensnared in the toils of duality. Right here is where we must be alert. We have experienced the liberty of the realization that we *are* the Christ. We know that the Christ is our *only* Identity. But this is not all. We know that the Christ is the Identity of everyone in existence. We certainly do not claim any more of the Christhood for ourselves than we attribute to everyone. Someone has made the statement to the effect that when we can look upon the face of the devil and see God, we have reached an understanding of God. This statement is not verbatim, but it is indeed meaningful. It is necessary for us to see God identified, no matter how opposite to that which is God anyone may appear to be.

We seem to be tempted on every side to accept something or someone that is not God. It may be well for us to occasionally remind ourselves that even the temptation to recognize and accept something that is not God is completely false and without any basis in fact.

> Let no man say when he is tempted, I am tempted of God: for God cannot be tempted with evil, neither tempteth he any man (Jas. 1:13).

There is no God in the temptation to accept duality. Neither is there any God in yielding to this fictitious appearance. God is neither the tempter nor the tempted. Only because God *is* can we be, so what could we be if we were not God being? This being true, we are neither the temptation nor the one tempted. This whole appearance of otherness is fictitious.

We do not accept as genuine any appearance of an evil power, an evil person, or an evil condition. We honor God and God alone. We do this by standing fast in the face of every appearance of another presence or power apart from God and by persisting in our awareness that God alone exists. Our constant criterion must be: "Is this God?" If It is God, It has to be good. If it is God, It has to be Love, Intelligence, Principle, and All that God is. If it is not God, it simply does not exist, and we cannot be tempted to accept it, to honor it, or to believe it.

We do not run away from those appearances of evil any more than Moses ran away from the rod that appeared to be a serpent. Never was that rod a serpent. Never was the rod anything other than a rod. Moses did not ignore the appearance of a serpent. On the contrary, he faced right up to it and actively saw through its pretense. Then it was that the true nature of the rod became apparent to Moses.

No doubt that illusory serpent *appeared* very real and very active to Moses. It must also have seemed to have intelligence, at least enough to harm or destroy him. Even though Moses seemed to experience great fear, he refused to run away from the illusion. Neither did he ignore it.

Rather, he became very active, and his activity was proof that he was not afraid. He is recorded to have "put forth his hand, and caught it, and it became a rod in his hand" (Exod. 4:4).

This experience of Moses, whether it is considered to be genuine or symbolical, should be an inspiring and enlightening example for us. We do not run away from any appearance of a presence or power other than God. Neither do we ignore it. We too become very active, and our activity is fearlessly facing the so-called illusion. We grasp—and realize—the fact that God *is* All that is, or can be, present.

We cannot partially accept the fact that God is All. We cannot say that God is All there is of us and not realize that God is All there is of the Universe, the World, of Everything and Everyone.

If we accept and entertain any illusion of duality regarding the world, we are going to appear to experience this same falsity in our daily lives and experience. Furthermore, if we are deluded by duality, we are going to appear to experience something that is not God in, or as, our Bodies. This is inevitable because our entire Existence is comprised of just that which we accept, recognize, and honor. Our experience is not something separate from the world experience. Our daily lives are not separate from the lives of everyone in existence. Our Bodies are not something separate from, or other than, our Consciousness.

Thus, whatever we entertain in our Consciousness *must* be apparent in and as our daily affairs, our experiences, and our Bodies. If we submit to an illusion of any kind, we will seem to encounter illusion in our experience. This does not make the illusion genuine. Nothing can make an illusion be anything other than the nothingness it is. But if we seem to be deluded by duality, an illusion can certainly seem real to us.

During our period of study and contemplation, it is so easy to perceive the genuineness of Perfection and the nothingness of imperfection. It is so very clear that God really *is* All and that All really *is* God. But then we come out from our study and someone turns on the television set, or we read a headline, or someone calls our attention to an apparent contradiction to every Truth we have just been perceiving. Our first reaction is to constantly refute this contradiction, silently of course, and go joyously about our daily affairs.

Then perhaps something will appear that pertains to one of our loved ones; or it may be that some difficulty may appear as our own experience. This is the moment to be on the alert because here a *personal* illusion is involved. Of course, we cannot deny the so-called evil and affirm the Truth. We cannot do anything that would involve the assumptive human mind in the least. But if our Consciousness remains completely stayed on the Allness that is God, we will not be caught unaware, and we will not even be tempted to accept false evidence.

When we are confronted with *any* illusion of duality, we should constantly remind ourselves of the salient facts which are genuine. In this way, we are actively facing up to the illusionary appearance. We do not do any mental work to change the appearance of duality or to get rid of it. We just let this false appearance remind us of that which is true and genuine. Any appearance of duality can instantly remind us of the fact that God is the one and only Existence. Should there be an illusion of hatred, we are reminded to rejoice in the Omnipresence which is infinite, eternal, uninterrupted Love. Should there be a falsity called egotism, we can realize at once that God is the only *I.* If the news of the day should present a picture of a threat to all Life, we can be instantly aware of the fact that God is the *only* Life, and God is never in danger.

No matter what false picture may be presented to us, we can instantly remind ourselves of the everlasting fact: God is the only Life, Substance, Consciousness, Love, Intelligence. No matter what the specific aspect of duality may seem to be, we should always realize the presence of Omniaction right here and right now. It is utterly impossible to contemplate Omniaction, or God in action, without a tremendous sense of the All-Presence being the *only* One and the *only* One acting.

It is well to remind ourselves that there is no temptation to believe in duality. God really *is* the only Mind, and the Mind that is God knows naught of anything other than Itself. Now, then, could the one and only Mind be tempted to accept another presence or power? God being the only Intelligence, you have to be the Intelligence which is God; otherwise, you could not be the intelligence that could even raise a finger or blink an eye. Therefore, if God be not tempted to recognize another presence or power, you are not tempted to believe another presence or power. There is no one that is really tempted, and there is nothing that can really tempt you to accept the illusion of duality.

Thus it is that we stand fast in the complete liberty, freedom, which is eternally established as our own Christ-Identity. Never do we waver. Never are we tempted to accept, honor, or believe in a presence or a power that is not the Presence and Power of God. Never do we attribute Intelligence to a seemingly destructive mind which would claim to enslave. Never do we accept that *any* so-called element of this Universe has power, or is power, that can be destructive.

We accept and honor God, and *only* God. We accept and honor *only* the Intelligence which is infinite Love. We accept and honor *only* the activity of this loving Intelligence. We accept and honor *only* the omniactive, perfect, conscious, living, loving Intelligence that *is* God.

This, dear One, is the omniactive, perfect, conscious, living, loving Intelligence which is your free Christ-Identity.

Questions and Answers

Q: Is it necessary to experience illumination in order to be healed?

A: Of course, we know that the word *healed* is not exactly right in this context. But the student who sent in this question also knows there is never anything in need of healing. It was just that the word *healed* enabled her to put her question more succinctly.

There is no Consciousness that is not illumined, or enlightened. It is not always apparent as illumination. But Life Itself *is* the Light, and this Light is the Consciousness of every Identity in Existence. It is not necessary to consciously experience that aspect of illumination which is seeing and being the Universe of Light. It *is* necessary to acknowledge that God is the Completeness, the Entirety, the Allness that constitute the Universe, the Identity, and the Body. If there could be a completely unillumined Consciousness, this phantasm could not accept or acknowledge the Allness which is God.

Never deny your illumined God-Consciousness, for it takes the Consciousness that is already enlightened to recognize and acknowledge the Allness which is God. Even though it may appear that you are not completely aware of being illumined Consciousness, just recognize the fact that in order to be conscious at all, you must be conscious as the illumined God-Consciousness. Never need anyone doubt the power of the Presence of Perfection just because he has not consciously, as yet, experienced full illumination.

Boundless Freedom

What is this mortal being,
So tightly circled 'round?
What is this mortal seeing?
With what can it be bound?
Can living, loving, conscious Mind
Be bound? Is God not All?
Can boundless freedom be defined,
Enclosed, as by a wall?

Oh, living, loving, boundless One,
The birthless, deathless *I*,
Oh, Light more luminous than the Sun,
There's nothing to deny
Thy unconfined Identity
Which e'er remains the same,
For this is Thy Divinity,
And I AM is Thy Name.

Light and Love,
Marie S. Watts

August 1963

In the beginning was the Word, and the Word was with God, and the Word was God.

—John 1:1

Dear One,

Every day brings more glorious reports of your own revelations. Of course, this does not mean that the Truth you perceive is separated. But it is truly an inspiring experience to receive your letters telling of your greater and more frequent revelations of the universal indivisible Truth.

I note that many of you are writing poetry. This is wonderful! There is an obvious rhythm and flowing activity in poetry, and it is axiomatic that this Omniaction should be apparent as free-flowing, rhythmic expression. I also note that your revelations are often expressed in prose. But it is such beautiful prose.

So many of you have sent page after page of your glorious revelations. Always, my heart sings when I see how gloriously the Beauty that is God is fulfilling Its purpose. Again and again, I find myself saying, "Yes, oh yes, this Identity is the Revelator and the Revelation." This is the basic Truth. The revelation and the revelator are the *same One*. All there is of any Identity is the Revelator, God, revealing Itself, *being* Its own Revelator, as Its own revelation.

Now, once in a while, one of you will write that you seem to have slipped back a little. Don't you believe it! Have you ever climbed a mountain? If you have, no doubt you have had the same experience most of us have had. Sometimes the ascent will be quite steep, and when it is, we know we are climbing rapidly toward the view at the top. Then suddenly we may step on some loose shale or something like that. We may even slip back a few steps. But we never lose our awareness of our goal, and *the seeming slip downwards only serves to enable us to discover a more secure footing.* We do not become discouraged; neither do we criticize ourselves for accidentally stepping in the loose shale. Rather, we simply take a deep breath, look the situation over, and *place our feet on a more firm foundation.* Generally we find ourselves climbing faster because we seemed to have slipped back a little.

Thus it is with us. Although any simile must of necessity be faulty, we can consider the foregoing as a basis for our seeming climb toward complete illumined Existence. Of course, we realize that actually we are not doing anything of ourselves. We know that it is all God announcing more completely Its infinitely glorious Self to be our *only* Self. At least for a while, it does *seem* as though we are striving. But never mind, your enlightened Consciousness must inevitably reveal that never have you been anywhere but at the top of the mountain.

Indeed, *never have you been any other than the complete enlightened One.* If God be All, who or what could you be if you were not God, being God? Illumination reveals that the climb and the struggle, even the seeming discouraging delay, never really happened. Rather, it has been God all the while. *Always and in all ways, it is God.* It is God revealing, God announcing, God identifying, and God evidencing Itself. *This is your only Self.*

There is a point beyond the seeming pitfalls of the illusory ascent. Many of you know this to be true because you are walking as illumined Beings. It is only now that you can fully realize the wonderful Truth that you never really went through the "trial and error" period at all. You may even wonder how you could have been so disturbed and sometimes distraught by such delusions. But you have infinite compassion for those who have not yet quite realized constant enlightenment. *You know how real it seemed.* Furthermore, you know that it seems just as real to anyone who does not yet appear to live and move and have his Being as an illumined Identity.

It is always inspiring to consider Jesus and his great understanding of the seeming needs and weaknesses of assumptive man. He walked around as a completely illumined Being. Yet he could understand how genuine *seemed* to be the suffering of the people. He was, and is, Love Itself. This fact was evidenced as his great compassion. It is noteworthy that he never rebuked anyone for seeming to be ill or to be blind to the glory that is, yet he knew that they were neither ill nor blind. But he understood. And I am convinced that without his great compassion he could not have been the tremendous Power that he manifested so beautifully. Indeed, Jesus did "walk around in the dream awake," but he loved. *Oh, how he loved!* He knew what it was to be infinite, impersonal, immeasurable Love.

Thus it must be with us. We too live and move and have our Being as illumined Identities. But we too understand. We know that it was only yesterday that we seemed to be immersed in dreams. In fact, we may even have seemed to awaken from a nightmare. So we love. We have compassion. Never do we rebuke anyone. Rather, we speak and act lovingly because we *are* Love. It is Love that is the Power of our *seeing* and of our Being.

Compassion

The word *compassion* may be defined in many ways. Yet underlying all the definitions there is one all-important word. This word is *Love*. To be compassionate means to really *be* Love. To be Love means to be Intelligence because

Love and Mind are inseparably One. Intelligent Love loves intelligently. Thus, intelligent Love is *intelligently* compassionate. True compassion is Love being intelligently loving. Let us observe intelligent Love in action and perceive just how It functions.

First of all, it is necessary to realize that eternal Perfection is a forever established Principle. It does not vary, neither does It waver. There is nothing in existence which can change this forever established Principle—Perfection. Even omnipotent Love cannot change *apparent* imperfection. Infinite Love knows nothing of imperfection. So it would be impossible for the activity of infinite Love to change or improve that which already is perfect. Therefore, the purpose of intelligent Love is not to change anything or even to heal anything. Yet paradoxically, it is when the Consciousness is surging in and *as* infinite Love that the Perfection which *is* becomes immediately evident.

The Bible says:

> There is no fear in love, but perfect love casteth out fear because fear hath torment. He that feareth is not made perfect in love (1 John 4:18).

The foregoing quotation is a very clear statement of Absolute Truth. Love is completely free of fear because Love has no awareness of anything to fear. Perfect Love is Love aware only of *being* Absolute Perfection. Furthermore, it is intelligent Love aware of *seeing* and *knowing* only Perfection. If there seems to be the least appearance of fear, there must also appear to be something or someone to fear. This would mean that we were aware of a presence and a power that was not God, who is immutable, eternal Perfection. It is perfect Love that reveals the presence of the glorious Perfection which does exist despite any nightmarish *appearance* of imperfection.

Any appearance of inharmony is an illusion that imperfection exists. It makes no difference whether the illusion be one of ill health, lack, mental turmoil, or whatever; the false appearance seems to signify the presence of imperfection. Yet God *is* All, so Perfection *is* All. This being true, All is Perfection. This means that Perfection is the only Presence, and Perfection is the *only* Essence and Activity that can be known to be present.

Sometimes we are faced with an appearance of imperfection which seems very real. This is particularly true if the difficulty seems to be the experience of one whom we love greatly. Right here is where we find it necessary to be very sure that our compassion is intelligent Love in action. It is omniactive, intelligent Love which reveals the evidence of the Perfection that has been right here all the while.

The Love which Jesus was, and is, was equally compassionate, whether It was evidenced in his perception of the one he called mother or whether It was evidenced in his perception of the multitude. You are familiar with the following two episodes in the experience of the one called Jesus. His compassion—intelligent Love—was equally evidenced in each of these experiences.

For instance, Jesus had compassion when he observed the multitude that had followed him into the wilderness. He knew that they appeared to need food. Jesus needed no food. Neither was he aware of hunger. But this did not mean that he was not aware of the seeming need of the multitude. This is an example of intelligent Love in action. Yet it was this same Love in action which recognized the seemingly tragic grief of the one he called mother.

When Mary stood before the cross upon which Jesus, her son, was supposed to be crucified, she evidently did not speak of the grief that seemed so real to her. To Mary, it must have seemed that her son was faced with great suffering and that his death was inevitable. Jesus was aware of her seeming mental suffering and turmoil, yet he was not suffering, mentally or otherwise, He knew that he could neither suffer nor die. Yet he had compassion. He recognized that which *seemed* to be the need of the one he called mother.

> When Jesus therefore saw his mother, and the disciple standing by, whom he loved, he saith unto his mother, Woman, behold thy son! Then saith he to the disciple, Behold thy mother! And from that hour that disciple took her unto his own home (John 19:26-27).

It is noteworthy that Jesus did not address Mary as "Mother." He knew so well that human birth and death are illusory experiences. Yet he knew that to Mary he was her son, and he also knew what her need seemed to be. Furthermore, he presented to her the son which it *seemed* to her she must lose. The statement "behold thy son" is fraught with spiritual meaning. But one must be aware of the birthless, deathless nature of each Identity if the full significance of this statement is to be apparent. Our purpose, at the moment, is to observe the compassion which is intelligent Love in action.

Jesus was not one to hide his head in the sand. He knew that inharmony, trouble, sickness, sin, and death *appeared* to be present. Yet he was his own immunity to all of these fallacious appearances. His immunity did not hinder his compassionate understanding of those who did not yet realize their immunity to these false appearances. How great was his compassion and understanding when Mary Magdalene, the supposed sinner, was brought before him. He knew so well that both the sin and the sinner were but an illusion's illusion. Yet his pure seeing evidently revealed the genuine purity of her own Nature. This is evident from the fact that the whole illusion of sin was dispelled in her experience.

Every so-called healing that Jesus was said to perform transpired because he first perceived the seeming nature of the illusion, and yet he was the intelligent Love which dispelled the illusion. For instance, he recognized the fact that Lazarus *seemed* to have died. In fact, he had told the disciples that Lazarus was dead. Yet Jesus knew that there was no death. Had he not known this Truth, he could not have presented Lazarus alive and well to those standing before the tomb.

It is recorded in the Bible that Jesus wept just before he told Lazarus to "come forth." He could not have wept because he believed Lazarus had died. Oh, no. He wept because they—the sisters of Lazarus and the bystanders—seemed to be so blind. No wonder Jesus wept. His immunity could not be their immunity. But his compassion could and did reveal the incontrovertible fact that the Life of Lazarus was deathless, eternal, and his Body was imperishable. Jesus could not perceive this tremendous Truth *for* others. He knew that *each Identity must be his own Revelator*. But the great Love which was manifested as Jesus could and did reveal the Truth he knew, as the evidence of Perfection.

We have often quoted the statement that "He walked around in the dream awake." This is very much the way it was with this intelligent, compassionate One. Although he knew that God—Life, Consciousness, Intelligence, Love—was all that ever could be present, Jesus also knew that this glorious Truth was not clearly perceived by others as yet. He knew that their illusions seemed real to them. But the most important fact of his great spiritual perception was that he *knew just what their illusions seemed to be*. It was very much like standing beside one who was asleep and having a dream, or even a nightmare, and knowing what the nightmare was presenting.

Thus it is with us. We too walk around in the dream awake. We too are aware that we cannot perceive the Absolute Presence of God as All *for* anyone. Oh yes, we too could sometimes weep. How Jesus must have yearned to lovingly say to those who seemed to be deluded: *Just open your eyes and behold the glory that is God, revealed and manifested as All*. But if this most loving One could go all the way in his seeing and being omniactive Love, surely we cannot complain if we too are required to go all the way.

When the glory of the word *Love* is fully understood, there will be no false evidence called birth, death, sickness, pain, or inharmony of any kind. Neither will there be wars or threats of war. Compassion is an integral aspect of perfect Love. Compassion does not mean that we descend into the illusion, believe in it, or honor it in any way. Compassion does mean that we understand how real the nightmare *seems* to the apparent dreamer, and we do maintain our immunity to any illusion. In this way *only* can we emulate Jesus and his wonderful works. In this way *only* can we too be the Light to those who *seem*, at the moment, to be in darkness.

Yet we must always be aware that the genuine and *only* Identity of anyone is infinite, conscious, living, loving Intelligence and that each Identity must of necessity be this fully awake Intelligence. This is a paradox and not always easy to understand. But by perceiving this Truth, we experience the evidence of this Truth. Thus, although we do perceive the dreamless nature of each Identity, we have compassion because an Identity may have *seemed* to become temporarily unaware of his genuine and only Identity.

Thus it is, and thus it must be at the moment. But we *know* complete enlightenment is *inevitable*; no Identity can exist without *being* this Light, and the Light cannot forever be concealed. So let loving compassion intelligently be evident in and as our Consciousness. Let the seeming illusion be depleted and dissolved by the living, loving Light we *are* and know ourselves to be.

The Fallacy of Time

In the miasma called human existence, time is the great deceiver. It enters into and plays its mesmeric part in every event of the entire world of illusion. Yet there actually is no time. Those of you who experience illumination know there is no time, and the physicists, including those who are engaged in the space activity, are beginning to discover that *time is simply a word.* Furthermore, the word *time* is used to describe or discuss something which does not exist.

It is not surprising that the fallacy of time should seem to have so successfully deluded us. In the mass illusion of human life, there seems to be irrefutable evidence of time. Every event of the world of appearance seems to be measured by time. Every event of the illusory human experience seems to be measured by time.

Among the definitions of the word *time*, we find the following in Webster's unabridged dictionary:

> Time: The period during which an action, process, or the like, continues; the interval between leaving and returning; beginning and ending, etc.

This underlying deception is the measuring rod of all human life, and the above definition makes it apparent that the entire basis of time is beginning and ending. It appears to take time for the seasons to come and go. The illusory world would say it seems to take time for the tree to grow from the seed. It seems to take time for the fruit to appear on the tree. Then it seems to take time for the fruit to disappear and for the tree to become denuded of its fruit and of its beauty.

Yet despite all of this appearance, illumination always reveals the presence of the *complete* tree. Whenever, in illumination, the tree is seen, the seed, the roots, the trunk, the branches, and the leaves are gloriously present. Furthermore, if the tree should be fruitful, the full ripe fruit is on the tree, and any tree that blossoms also shows forth complete with blossoms.

Now, it is obvious that one or the other of these perceptions must be false. If the tree does grow from the seed, and if the leaves, the blossoms, and the fruit do appear and disappear, then the tree that is seen in illumination must be fictitious. Conversely, if the complete tree that is seen in illumination is genuine, then a temporary tree must be fictitious. Either the complete tree exists eternally, or the tree begins, changes, vacillates between completeness and incompleteness, and then ends. If the eternal tree is genuine, there can be no time. If the tree is temporal, there must be time. Let us explore this word *time* and see whether or not it has any genuine meaning.

The Bible presents, concisely and clearly, the difference between time and eternity:

> To everything there is a season, and a time to every purpose under the heaven: A time to be born, and a time to die; a time to plant, and a time to pluck up that which is planted; A time to kill, and a time to heal; a time to break down, and a time to build up; A time to weep, and a time to laugh … A time to get, and a time to lose … A time to love, and a time to hate; a time of war, and a time of peace (Eccles. 3:1-4, 6, 8).

Isn't this a gloomy picture? It is small wonder that the Preacher felt so discouraged and so hopeless:

> What profit hath he that worketh in that wherein he laboureth? (Eccles. 3:9).

Yes, one wonders what point there would be in existing if our entire existence must be governed by a measuring rod called time.

Obviously the Preacher was not illumined when he wrote these disheartening words. He was apparently deceived by the very illusion which he was so persistently presenting. He was judging genuine Existence by a false measuring rod.

Oh my, where is God in all of this sorry picture? *Nowhere*! Is not God eternal? Is not God All? Is not All God? Does the Allness which is God begin and end? Does the Allness which is God live and die, love and hate, war and make peace? No! Does the Allness which is God come to fruition and then deteriorate? Does the Allness that is God gain and lose? No! *The immutable Completeness which is God remains eternally perfect and complete.*

Jesus knew that time did not exist. His perception of Eternity was diametrically opposite to the misconception of the unillumined Preacher. He knew that the seedtime and the harvest were not divided and measured by an illusion called time. You will remember that he said:

> Say not ye, There are yet four months and then cometh harvest? Behold, I say unto you, Lift up your eyes and look on the fields; for they are white already to harvest (John 4:35).

The illumined One called Jesus saw that which is here, and he saw it the way it was and is. This is the way the Universe and all Existence is seen by everyone who experiences what we will call visual illumination.

The immutable Eternality which is God precludes the possibility of time. The conscious, living Intelligence which is God can have no awareness of time. Actually, there is no genuine consciousness of time because that which is unknown to God must be infinitely unknown. God is the *only* conscious Mind. God is the *only* conscious, intelligent Life. So there can be no conscious, living mind that knows anything of time.

This is a complete Universe. God *is* this Universe. All that God is, is God *right now*. God can never become God. Neither can God cease to be God. God cannot become All because God has never ceased to be All. God is the tree, the seed, the leaf, and the blossom, and God is present right now. Thus, God is the leaf, the seed, and the blossom right now. This being true, how could there be a time when there was no leaf and no blossom?

It is the illusion of time which makes the seed appear to be necessary before the complete tree is in existence. It is an illusion of time which makes it appear that the leaves, the blossoms, and the fruit begin and end. It is the illusion of time which makes it appear that there are "yet four months and then cometh harvest."

It is the illusion of time that makes it appear that we have birthdays. It is the illusion of time that makes it appear that we have death days. It is the illusion of time which makes it appear that we can be incomplete today and hope to be complete tomorrow, next week, or next year. It is the illusion of time that makes it appear that we can be in lack today and look forward to abundance at some future date. It is the illusion of time that makes it appear that we can be imperfect today but perhaps we will be perfect in some uncertain future time.

When is God not All? Is not God the Essence, the Form, and the Activity of Everything and Everyone in existence right now? God is completely perfect, for God is Perfection and God is complete. Every aspect of God is complete right now. Every aspect of God is completely perfect right now. There is nothing in existence that is not God being That. But *God can only be God*. So *God being That is God being God.*

Every aspect of God is Perfection being perfect. There is no time in which Perfection can lapse into imperfection. Neither is there a time in which illusory imperfection can become perfect. Perfection is. Imperfection is not. There is no time in which an effect from a nonexistent illness could maim, cripple, or weaken your Body. There is no time in which you were born, matured, and aged. There is no time in which you suffered. There is no time in which you sinned. There is no time in which you can become any more perfect than you are right now. How can complete Perfection become more perfect? There is no time in which you can become any more free than you are right now. Neither is there any time in which you can become any more pure than you are right now.

It is impossible to conceive of a time in which God was anymore or any less God. Neither can you imagine God-Identity to be any more or any less God. God is the *Eternal Now*. God is the *Infinite Here*. You exist *Now*. You exist *Here*. You exist because God is All there is of You right Here and Now. There is no time *Now*. There is no time *Here*. So there is no time existing in or *as* the Hereness, the Nowness, of your Existence.

Oh, beloved One, an entire book could be written on the Presence of timeless, spaceless Completeness. This book would have to explore every aspect of the Completeness which *is* God.

Be your own explorer. Let the Consciousness you have and *are* explore this glorious, perfect, eternal, infinite Universe. You can, you know, because It is already established within and as *Your own Consciousness*. It does not take time for you to explore your Self. Neither does it take time for your infinite, indivisible Self to be revealed. *You are It and It is You*. Best of all, it is the fact that *You know your Self to be what you are, and you do not know your Self to be what you are not.* Thus does the Hereness and the Nowness of your Self reveal Itself.

Questions and Answers

Q: Does perfect vision imply seeing matter perfectly?

A: Matter cannot be seen. Matter does not exist, so it would be impossible to actually see it. Even the physicists are aware of this fact. That which is called matter consists of an illusion's essence in form. An illusion has to be the only essence, form, and activity of its own self-deceived existence. No one can actually see an illusion. Therefore, it would be impossible to see matter perfectly or to see perfect matter.

Even the substance of the eye that *seems* to see matter is illusory. You see, the human eye is one aspect of the whole illusion that there is an identity called man, born of human flesh and dependent upon his human body for its existence. In fact, it would make it appear that the identity was powerless to be alive, conscious, or intelligent if he did not live in a human body. A human body is said to be matter. It is not matter, for there is no matter. It cannot be Mind, because Mind is not visible to the illusory human eye. It cannot be both Mind *and* matter, because the presence of one precludes the possibility of the presence of the other. We know that Mind, Consciousness, Life exist. So that which is called matter cannot be genuine. It really cannot exist.

Perfect Vision does see Perfection, but It does not see perfect matter. Perfect Vision is perfect, conscious perception. It is actually God seeing. It has to be Perfection because God can only perceive Himself. Perfect Vision sees perfectly. It is limitless, and It is indivisible. Consciousness cannot be divided into Consciousnesses. Thus it is that

Vision cannot be divided into visions. Perfect Consciousness is perfect Perception. Perfect Perception is perfect Vision. Perfect Vision is equally present in and as the Vision of each and every one of us.

There is never any more or any less Vision. Neither can Vision fluctuate. Never is It interrupted. Never is It subject to illusory matter for Its completeness. Neither is It dependent upon eyes of matter for Its perfect activity. Perfect Vision is Spirit seeing. But Spirit is Consciousness, so the Vision that exists sees the Consciousness It *is*, in form and in action. Thus perfect Vision is omniactive, living Consciousness, perfectly perceiving Its own omnipresent Perfection.

Compassionate Love

When Mary stood before the cross,
So filled with anguish at the loss
Of her beloved Son,
How real her trouble must have seemed,
How grievous the event she deemed
Must mean the death of One
Whose life had but begun
To be fulfilled.

But he "had risen" and the cross
Could hold no threat of pain or loss,
For life had ne'er begun;
The risen Christ didst know the way,
To one called mother he could say,
Of yet another one,
"Woman, behold thy son."
'Twas Love fulfilled.

Light and Love
Marie S. Watts

September 1963

In the beginning was the Word, and the Word was with God, and the Word was God.

—John 1:1

Dear One,

Those of you who attended our seminar are well aware of the indescribable glory of that event. Many of you who did not attend were intensely aware of the tremendous enlightenment that was being revealed. Some of you "tuned in," and the letters telling of your revelations are paeans of joy. I can assure you that we also rejoice in this further proof that Consciousness, be It infinite or specific, is boundless, indivisible, and immeasurable.

It may be interesting to you to know that before we started each session, we had a few moments of silent contemplation. During those moments, we were fully aware of the indivisible nature of our Consciousness and that the Consciousness we were, and are, was the very same Consciousness that you are. We realized that our revelations were not confined to the lecture hall, to Hollywood, to California, or to the United States. We were aware that the One Consciousness, revealing Itself, was conscious infinitely and eternally, and that this one complete Consciousness was conscious as you, as us, and as everyone in existence. It is not surprising that so many of you who were "apparently" absent experienced such great illumination. As for those of us who were there, we know that there are no words with which we can describe the power of the Presence and the presence of the Power that was revealed. We know that the seminar did not end.

There is one important aspect of our revelations I must share with those of you who were unable to attend. This is important because it brings into clear focus the basic premise of the Ultimate. This premise is that within and *as* the Consciousness of every Identity, there does exist every Truth that can ever be revealed. Consequently, each one of us is his own revelator and his own revelation. There can be no teacher and no leader in the Ultimate. Even though we have classes, we are alertly aware of the fact that this Truth is not being taught to anyone.

During the last three days and nights of the seminar, there were many evidences that the Truths that were to be spoken had *already* been revealed within and as the Consciousness of some of you who attended. In fact, often the very sequence of the words was the same as those that were spoken a moment or two later from the platform. One enlightened One reported that she really heard the words just before they were spoken, and that when they were spoken, it was very much like an echo of the words she had heard.

We were so very conscious of being the One Consciousness, One Life, One Intelligence, One Love that it is not surprising that the revelations being experienced in and as Consciousness should be consciously present within and as the Consciousness of the specific Identity, whether or not they had been spoken. Right here is our proof that there can be no higher or lower, no greater or lesser, no more or no less of Truth existing as each and every one of us. Thus, there can be no leader or follower and no revelator other than the Consciousness of the One who experiences the revelation.

This is why I rejoice so very much when you inform me that you are experiencing your own revelations. Indeed, "Thou art not far from the kingdom of God" (Mark 12:34). How could you be far from the kingdom, Consciousness, of

God when God is your own Consciousness? And once the fallacious little self-important "I" is no longer apparent, the kingdom, Consciousness, is aware of being complete. To be complete Consciousness means to be complete Intelligence. Complete Intelligence is the Infinite Mind which knows Itself to *be* every Truth in existence. And of course, that all-important aspect called Love is eternally omnipresent.

This is the Consciousness you have and are. This is the only Consciousness of everyone who is conscious. Our last seminar was the most powerful proof of this Truth that we have yet experienced and evidenced, and we do rejoice in this awareness.

Since the seminar, I have been almost constantly in contemplation, and that which has been—and is being—revealed cannot yet be spoken or written in words. Yet I know that the words will appear when the revelations should be given. Thus, I wait and listen. Perhaps you too are experiencing these same tremendous revelations. If so, you will know them before they are ever expressed in words. Because we *know* our Oneness, we can expect the revelations of one of us to be the revelations of all of us. And thus it is.

The First Commandment

A contemplative study of the first and second commandments from the standpoint of the Ultimate will reveal many Truths which may not have been perceived previously.

> And one of the scribes came, and having heard them reasoning together, and perceiving that he had answered them well, asked him, Which is the first commandment of all?
>
> And Jesus answered him, The first of all the commandments is, Hear, O Israel, The Lord our God is one Lord: And thou shalt love the Lord thy God

> with all thy heart, and with all thy soul, and with all thy mind, and with all thy strength: this is the first commandment.
>
> And the second is like, namely this, Thou shalt love thy neighbor as thyself. There is none other commandment greater than these (Mark: 28-31).

It is noteworthy that the word *love* appears so prominently in both the first and the second commandments. But of equal importance is the fact that Jesus' first statement in answer to the scribe declared the Oneness, the Allness, and the Onliness which is God. To "love God with all thy heart" means to let all the Love that you know and *are* be the Love that is God. This is true because the genuine purpose and function of the Heart is Love. In fact, the entire spiritual significance of the Heart is impersonal, infinite, eternal, immutable Love. To love God means to *be* the Love which is God. God *is* Love, and there is no Love that is not God being Love.

We know that Jesus was aware that God was not a Presence or Power separate and apart from his own Being. You will remember that he said, "I and my Father are one" (John 10:30). We also know that Jesus did not reserve for himself alone the privilege of saying, "I and my Father are one." This fact is evident by Jesus' statement:

> That they all may be one; as thou, Father, art in me, and I in thee, that they also may be one in us … And the glory which thou gavest me I have given them, that they may be one, even as we are one (John 17:21-22).

It is true that Jesus was speaking primarily of the disciples. But are not we also the very Presence of the Christ? These wonderfully revealing words of Jesus were spoken not only for the disciples, but also for each and every Identity who is sufficiently enlightened to realize that he is the very same Oneness that Jesus evidenced as the Christ. Actually, these words were spoken for everyone in existence.

This is true, even though few there are who are aware of their tremendous spiritual significance.

Jesus was well aware of the fact that Love is of paramount importance in the realization of our oneness. Often we hear someone speak of being one *with* God. Right here, in this expression, is dualism. If we could be one *with* God, we would have to be something or someone separate from God, even though we were one *with* God.

It is like saying, "I am one with Nature, but I and Nature are two." The feeling of being one with Beauty is more as though we had an affinity for Beauty. But Oneness does not mean being one *with* God, Beauty, Nature, or any aspect of God. It does not even mean being one with anyone else. It simply means what it expresses—Oneness.

If we are to perceive the full spiritual significance of the first and second commandments, we must first know the inseparable nature of God and the inseparable nature of everyone and everything. We are not going to know what it means to *be* Love until we are aware of the indivisible nature of God, who comprises this entire Universe. In this way only can we perceive our infinite, inseparable Nature, and it is in this perception that impersonal, indivisible Love is recognized.

So long as the dualistic misconception of Consciousness separated into consciousnesses, Life divided into lives, and Mind divided into minds continues, there is also going to be the fallacious argument that Love can be separated into loves. Love is as inseparable and boundless as is Life, Consciousness, Intelligence. Once we are aware of this fact, we can really know the true meaning of Love. Furthermore, we can realize that we *are* Love Itself.

To love God with the whole Heart means to *be* the impersonal, inseparable Love which *is* God and to refuse to accept or honor any other kind of so-called human love. It means to love as God loves because you are God being Love. It means to accept *nothing* that appears to be hateful or worthy of hatred. It means to be completely aware of the fact that everyone and everything in our Universe is exactly the same Love that we are. No matter how real unlovely traits in others may *appear* to be, we accept and honor *only* Life, Consciousness, Intelligence, Love.

We must impersonalize the seeming evil, even as we impersonalize the genuine Good, or God. We don't try to wrap our Love into a separate bundle and deliver it to a certain individual or a certain group of individuals. Neither should we try to separate certain ones from the Love we are and bestow upon them our seeming hatred. We do not have to love that which appears to be evil, whether it seems to be an evil person, an evil situation, or an evil condition of some kind. But we should love Life, Consciousness, Mind, Love, no matter how, where, or when It appears in and as our Universe. To love God with the whole Heart, Mind, and strength means to see nothing but God, to know nothing that is not God. Thus, we can be aware of nothing that we do not love.

Jesus gives us a wonderful cue as to why it is necessary to love Life, Mind, Consciousness, no matter how contrary to God the assumptive personality may seem to be. First, he states the necessity to love God supremely and wholly. This he calls the first commandment. Then he says, "And the second is like…." This statement is followed by his assertion of the necessity to "love thy neighbor as thyself."

Indeed, the second commandment is like the first commandment. In fact, spiritually perceived, the first and the second commandments mean the same thing:

> To really love God means to love everything and everyone. To really love everyone and everything means to love God.

It would be impossible to love God, to love everything and everyone, if we did not know the inseparability of all Existence. If we believed the fallacy that Life, Consciousness, Mind could be separated into lives, consciousnesses, minds, we would always see something or someone who was not worthy of being loved. Always we would be aware of someone who appeared to deserve our criticism, or even our hatred. This is why the first commandment stresses the Oneness that is God.

In *The Gospel According to Thomas*, we find Jesus saying, "Love thy brother as thy soul" (Saying 25). He knew that Soul is God, thus, Soul is indivisible. He knew that Soul, Consciousness, Spirit were synonymous, and he was really adjuring us to love our brother as our own Consciousness. The Consciousness that is aware of being Love *is* the Consciousness of our neighbor, our brother, and our own God-Self. So it is evident that there really is no other mind, soul, consciousness, or life to either love or to hate.

This is why seeming hatred seems to harm the one who hates. The only hatred there could be, if there were a mind capable of hatred, would have to be the very self of the one who hated. Someone has said, "I cannot afford to hate anyone because the price I have to pay is too high." This is a profound statement, even though it does assume that there can be another mind to deserve hatred.

All of us are aware of the fact that the so-called human emotion called hatred seems to be very destructive. But few there are who realize that an assumptive human mind that is deluded by hatred is in the process of its own destruction. It is wonderful to know that there is no such mind.

There is one important word given in the first commandment that has been largely overlooked. This word is *strength*. Jesus admonishes us to love God with all our strength. Strength implies power, and it is true that Love is Power. It is the Power of *being* Love Itself. I know of no one word so fraught with Power as is the word *Love*. But in order to be fully aware of the power of Love, it is essential to be strong in our conviction that Love *is* All, All is Love. There must be a strong, powerful conviction that we *are* the Consciousness that is Love and that the Consciousness that is Love is the *only* Consciousness in existence. We must realize that this conscious Love is indivisibly One and that there is no other. To love God, the All as All, with all our strength means to love God as all the power of our unshakable conviction that God is Love and Love is All *as* All.

There is a wonderful sequel to Jesus' statement of the first commandment:

> And the scribe said unto him, Well, Master, thou hast said the truth: for there is one God; and there is none other but he: And to love him with all the heart, and with all the understanding, and with all the soul, and with all the strength, and to love his neighbor as himself, is more than all whole burnt offerings and sacrifices. And when Jesus saw that he answered discreetly, he said unto him, Thou art not far from the kingdom of God (Mark 12:32-34).

Indeed, the scribe was not far from the kingdom, the Consciousness, which is God. Only the Mind which *is* God could know the tremendous spiritual significance of Jesus' statements. Truly there is but one God, and "there is none other than he." The Consciousness of the one called the scribe was aware of this Truth. No wonder Jesus knew that he was not far from being fully aware of his God-Identity. By this same token, you are not far from the kingdom of God either. In fact, the kingdom of God is your very own Consciousness.

It is your own awareness of Being. It is the Life you are, the Consciousness you are, the Mind you are, and above all, it is the Love you are. If this were not true, you would not understand one iota of the spiritual significance of the first and second commandments, which really are one basic commandment. But you do understand; you do perceive; you are conscious of the inviolate Truth Jesus presented; thus, you are aware of being the very Consciousness which *is* the kingdom of God, right here and right now.

The Fallacy Called Age

One of the most cruel of all human so-called laws is the illusion called old age. The ironic aspect of this fallacy is that there is no such law. Rather, that which is spuriously called a law of age is nothing but an accepted belief. Furthermore, the accepted belief can only be accepted by a kind of mind that does not even exist.

Today there seems to be a concerted effort to intensify the illusion of old age. Numerous insurance plans are advertised offering financial security for this supposedly inevitable experience. In addition to this, we have the federal government compelling the individual to prepare for this eventuality by compulsory payment of social security. And we know about the federal and state plans called old age security. There are many other ways in which the spurious beliefs of age are increasingly foisted upon us, but these few examples are sufficient to alert us to this mesmeric situation.

It is true that the majority of our people do seem to need such protection. So long as the illusion of birth and death continues, there will be those who seem to need some assistance when that cruel fallacy, old age, overtakes them. We would not deny them any assistance that seems necessary. But we should be very alert to the rapidly increasing illusion that an inactive, purposeless, helpless experience is inevitable.

Of course, we pay our social security, even as we pay our taxes, because this is the law of the land. We are law-abiding citizens. Yet we know that we are only rendering unto Caesar the things that are Caesar's. We do not have to succumb to the fallacies of old age in order to be law-abiding. We do not consider social security as a necessary insurance that is to help us when we can no longer be normally active. We know that this spurious state of affairs can never be. We consider the payment of social security as an investment, in the same way we would invest in real estate, apartments, stocks or bonds, or whatever. But never do we make any investment with the spurious notion that this investment is going to mean security for a period of inactivity and helplessness.

Now that we have explored somewhat the fallacious experience of "man with breath in his nostrils," let us perceive that which is true pertaining to the genuine and only Identity.

We know that old age has to be entirely spurious because there is no such thing as time in which to age. Our space fliers have discovered that there is no universal time clock. Their discoveries along this line certainly expose many of the myths about the so-called world and its people. We cannot pursue their discoveries in this article, other than to state that they know there is no time.

This is also quite an important fact for us to know. If there is no time, there can be no time in which to be born, to mature, to age, and to die. An entire book could be written on the subject of the timeless Universe Itself. For our purpose at the moment, it is sufficient to realize the universal fact that time is only an illusion of the assumptive human mind.

There are many aspects of the illusion that contribute to the fantasy called old age. Foremost among these illusory aspects is the suppositional event called birth. As we know, life, intelligence, consciousness is supposed to become apparent in the individual at birth. This first appearance of the individual is supposedly dependent upon the existence of a man-created, temporal body of matter. Having beginning, this body, if it were genuine at all, would inevitably have an ending. This temporal body is doomed from its very first inception. Thus, the very first requisite in the perception that old age, ending in death, is a falsity is the *realization* that a born body is but an illusion that seems to conceal the eternal, changeless, perfect Body. It certainly would not be intelligent for God, Mind, to engender the destruction of Its own Substance, Life, Consciousness, Mind. God *is* the only Mind, and Mind, being Intelligence, *acts* intelligently.

As stated before, the first requisite in the perception that old age is false is the unshakable conviction that birth is simply a deception. Starting from this basis, we can begin to realize why the Body does not really deteriorate, age, and die.

Does the foregoing seem unreasonable to you? It would not seem so unreasonable to many of the great physicists and physicians. Not long ago, an article appeared in many of our leading newspapers, and the famous physicist who wrote this article frankly stated that they could find no real reason why the body should deteriorate, age, and die. Actually, if either the physicists or the physicians really knew what constitutes the Body, they would also know that old age, deterioration, etc., are but accepted beliefs; consequently, they are completely unnecessary to those who refuse to accept them.

The eternal, birthless, changeless, ageless, perfect Body is constituted of Life, Consciousness, Mind—Intelligence

—Love. There is nothing other than living, conscious Mind; consequently, the Body has to be comprised of conscious, living Mind. Consciousness is an eternal Existent. Life is eternal, and Mind is eternal Intelligence. Conscious, living Intelligence cannot deteriorate, age, perish, or die.

There is nothing alive other than Life Itself. There is nothing conscious other than Consciousness, and there is nothing intelligent other than Mind. This being true, the only Substance that can be alive as the living Body has to be eternal, changeless, indestructible, and forever perfect. This is the Body of Light that has been and is being seen by innumerable enlightened ones. And the eternal Body of Light is your *only* Body.

Please be assured that the realization of the ageless Body does evidence itself as what *appears* to be a human body. It makes no difference how aged the false concept of body may *appear* to be, this evidence of eternal perfection begins to be apparent the very moment illumined Consciousness reveals the *only* Body. Once this Body of Light is apparent, there can no longer be any concern about a seemingly aging body. How can we be concerned about something that does not exist? We can't. We aren't. Neither do we try to improve a kind of body that does not exist. We are unconcerned about any so-called laws of age, etc., because we are aware of having and *being* the eternal, birthless, indestructible, imperishable Body of Light.

Our kingdom, Consciousness, is not of this world; thus, we are not subject to any fallacious beliefs, called laws, of this world. The Body can no more be subject to these illusory accepted beliefs than can the conscious, living Mind because the Body is comprised of the conscious, living Mind Itself. Thus, the Body manifests only the eternal Perfection which the living Mind is aware of being.

Oh, it is all so wonderful. You will notice that your step is freer, and your whole Body is more aware of being stronger and more pliable. Your friends will begin to notice that you are, to them, looking and acting so much younger. But you know what is taking place. You know that the eternal Body, comprised of conscious, living Mind, is evidencing Itself right where an illusory sense of body appears to be.

It is in this realization that we understand what the illumined Isaiah was perceiving when he joyously said:

> But they that wait upon the Lord shall renew their strength, they shall mount up with wings as eagles, they shall run, and not be weary, and they shall walk, and not faint (Isa. 40:31).

Indeed, Isaiah was right. There is no false sense of a burdensome body. There is only a wonderfully free Body whose strength can never be depleted and whose activity is never restricted.

This is your Body right here and right now. This very moment you can cease to be deluded by the illusions, accepted beliefs, called human laws. This moment you can know that your only Body is made of your eternal, perfect Consciousness. This moment you can realize that your immutable Body of Light has always been, and will always be, your *only* Body. Thus, It will be evident *as* your Body right here and right now.

Inherent within and as the Consciousness of each one of us is the conviction that age, deterioration, death are not right or normal. By this same token, we must inherently know that this triad of illusions is not inevitable. If this were not true, we would never have tried to postpone the "last enemy" or to keep the body as young as possible, as long as we possibly could. No so-called human effort can free us from the cruelty of age. The very so-called mind that makes the effort to overcome the beliefs of age is the mind that accepts these illusions and believes them to be inevitable.

The conscious, living Mind that is God has no awareness of age, decrepitude, or imperfection of any kind. The conscious, living Mind that is your Existence is also the existence of your Body. Therefore, if you are conscious of being eternal, immutable, and forever perfect, your Body has to be conscious of being eternal, immutable, and forever perfect. This is inevitable because your Body *is* the conscious, living Mind you *are*, aware of being what you are.

Beloved, *now* are you the very Presence of eternal, ageless, living, conscious, loving Mind. *Now* your eternal Body of Light is your *only* Body. *Now* are you completely free from every illusion pertaining to birth, age, decrepitude, death. *Now* is your Body aware of *being* the glorious Perfection which It has always been and will forever be.

Questions and Answers

Q: Since God is All and there is no dualism (God and man), who or what are you listening to when you listen in contemplation? Who is illumining you? Are you thinking you are a separate identity from God?

A: All illumination is Self-illumination. There is nothing that can be revealed *to* anyone. All that is ever revealed is the infinite Identity revealing Itself as Itself. We sometimes say, "All is infinite Mind, revealing Itself *to* Itself *as* Itself." Even so, the revelation is experienced within and *as* the Consciousness of the one who is contemplating.

When, in contemplation, you are consciously listening, you are listening to your own God-Consciousness. You do not seek the answer to any question, as though the answer were to be revealed *to* you. Rather, you are aware that the answer is already present in and as your own God-Consciousness. In fact, enlightenment reveals that the question of itself is nothing. The answer is all-important. If the answer were not already present, there would be no question. No one would ask a question about *nothing*.

You do reach a point where you no longer question. At this point, you simply maintain your Consciousness as "full open" awareness, knowing that any answer that should be realized at any moment is already present as your own Consciousness and is revealed at the moment when it is essential to be aware of the answer. In a way, you might say you come to the point where the *answer* is revealed rather than the question. But this takes place in great illumination.

It is true that the questions do seem to start the answers flowing. But as enlightened Consciousness, we reinterpret the questions, and in this reinterpretation, we really recognize the question to be the answer insisting upon being revealed or recognized.

If the questions seem necessary to the recognition of the omnipresent answers, we do not hesitate to question. But we never question with the misconception that the answer to the question is to be revealed from some source outside our own Consciousness. We know that, our Consciousness being infinite, *there is no outside*, and thus, there can be no source from which the answers can come *to* us. It is exceedingly important to realize that your infinite Consciousness is whole, entire, complete; thus, *there are no unanswered questions*. In this way, you will begin to realize that the *answer* is all that exists, and the question will no longer be of any importance.

The Omnipresent Splendor

I am the wind that sighs in the trees,
I am the leaf that sways in the breeze,
I am the ripple of the water that flows,
I am the luminous Beauty that glows,
The iridescent Splendor.

I am the rhythm of all moving things,
I am the song of the bird as it wings
Its effortless way in the spaceless skies;
I am the surge of the free-flowing tides,
The omniactive Splendor.

I am the beauteous, infinite One,
I am the heavens, the moon, the sun,
I am the Essence of all that exists,
I am the Presence of All that is,
The Omnipresent Splendor.

Light and Love,
Marie S. Watts

October 1963

In the beginning was the Word, and the Word was with God, and the Word was God.

—John 1:1

Dear One,

Shortly after you receive this issue of *The Word*, the boys and girls of your neighborhood will appear at your door saying, "Trick or treat." They will be wearing masks, and their Halloween costumes will be designed to complete the concealment of their identities. Some of these masks and costumes may be very beautiful, some may be ridiculous, and some of them may be definitely monstrous. These monstrous masks and costumes, of course, are supposed to terrify you.

A student of the Ultimate once told me of an experience she had one Halloween. She seemed to be faced with a problem that appeared to be very real and terrifying. Suddenly a boy appeared at her door. He was dressed and masked in one of those costumes. Apparently his disguise was particularly gruesome, because she was, just at first, quite taken aback at the apparition. Suddenly she penetrated the disguise and realized that this was a boy she knew very well. Furthermore, he was a fine lad and lived right next door. Then she found herself saying, "Why, this is no little monster. This is my fine little friend who lives next door." Needless to say, her perception of the genuine identity of the lad, despite the monstrous appearance, enabled her to draw an analogy between this seeming human experience and her own seeming monstrous problem.

All of us can be benefited by just such instances as the foregoing. No matter how real or how terrifying any *appearance* may seem to be, we can penetrate, see right through, the disguise and recognize the *actuality* right where the false appearance seems to be. We can refuse to be deceived. We can refuse to be mesmerized by any appearance of inharmony or abnormalcy. It makes no difference whether the false appearance pertains to business, the home, or the body. We do not concern ourselves with the fallacious *appearance*. We don't try to heal it or to change it. We just stand firm in our awareness of the Perfection that does exist, until the monstrous disguise is seen through. In this way, we perceive that which is true, and we also experience the evidence of that which has always been true.

Letters continue to come in telling of wonderful illuminations and revelations experienced during the seminar. This is only further proof of the boundless, indivisible, immeasurable nature of our revelations. It is truly wonderful to realize that our revelations are being revealed in and *as* the Consciousness of so many Identities. We can rejoice in every contemplation, knowing that our revelations are unconfined and as illimitable as is infinite Love Itself. Oh, the wonderful Love that flows and surges as our Consciousness in this unselfed contemplation.

I am so happy that those of you who attended the seminar are continuing with the questions given during the morning sessions. It is noteworthy you are now perceiving the paradoxical fact that the question of itself is nothing. It only signifies the presence of the answer insisting upon being revealed. There is only One to question, and that One is your own God-Consciousness. It is wonderful to know that the question and answer are inherent within and *as* the Consciousness of each one of us. We rejoice in the realization of our eternal completeness, as each day brings further proof of the boundless, perfect, living, loving, conscious Mind, which comprises all there is of us and all there is of All.

The Right and the Wrong Way of Questioning

There are three ways of questioning that are familiar to all of us along the spiritual path. Two of these ways are futile, and we can never discover satisfactory answers to our questions because they are based upon a false premise. Any question is futile that is based upon the assumption that something other than God exists. But there is one way of questioning that is right, and we can be very certain that the answers to these questions will be revealed. The right questions are based upon the premise that God is All, All is God.

Let us first discuss the questions that are based upon a false premise. All of us have asked these questions, and no one of us has ever discovered the answers to them. Again and again, we have asked, "If God is All, why does it even *seem* there is evil?" This is the first unanswerable question. The second question is similar in nature. All of us have asked, "With all the Truth I know, why does this evil appearance still persist?"

Of course, we ask these questions in different words and in various ways, but basically these futile questions are based upon the same premise—that evil exists and that it is genuine. Conversely, these questions reveal that the questioner is not wholly convinced that God *is* All, All *is* God.

All of us have said, "Oh, I know that these evil appearances are not real, but still they *seem* to exist. Then we have questioned as to why there seems to be the existence of something we have just said does not exist. Either a thing exists or it does not exist.

The word *seems* implies an appearance, or evidence, of something. All of us use this word, for want of a word that describes *nothing*. Yet there is no word that describes nothing except *nothing*. The more we try to explain the nothing called evil the more we make it appear to be "something."

When we question as to why something that does not exist *seems* to exist, we are really asking why nothing appears to be something. Thus, we are asking questions about nothing, while we are assuming this "nothing" to be "something." No one would knowingly ask questions about nonexistence. So the very fact that we question about evil means that, at least to some extent, we feel we are questioning about "something." Once we are wholly aware of the fact that evil really *is* nothing, we no longer are concerned with any fallacious appearance called evil.

Jesus said:

> Strait is the gate, and narrow is the way which leadeth unto life, and few there be that find it (Matt. 7:14).

Indeed, this is true. We walk in the direction in which we look. We turn neither to the appearance of evil nor to questioning about an appearance of nothing. We refuse to be diverted. We refuse to honor something that does not exist by questioning why it seems to exist. We keep our attention firmly established in the fact that God is All, All is God, and we *hold fast* to this absolute premise. We refuse to be double-minded. We refuse to be deluded by dualism. We refuse to be moved by the fallacy that something can appear, or be evident, that is not God.

In other words, we are aware of the peace that Isaiah was speaking of when he said:

> Thou wilt keep him in perfect peace, whose mind is stayed on thee: because he trusteth in thee (Isa. 26:3).

Yes, our Consciousness is so completely God-filled—God fulfilled—that we are not even tempted to question about something that is not God and thus cannot exist.

Now let us speak of the second question pertaining to "nothing." I am sure that every one of us has questioned as to why the Truth we knew did not dispel some appearance of evil. We have said, "Oh, I know this is not real, but how can it persist when I am knowing the Truth so clearly?" If we find ourselves questioning in this way, it would be well to deliberately ask ourselves whether or not we *really know* the Truth, and *only* the Truth. In fact, it would be well to ask ourselves just exactly what is the Truth that we really know.

Beloved, I am going to briefly share with you an experience that ended all questioning about "nothing" for me. I am sure it will be helpful to you also. Although my entire experience from what is called childhood had been a search for God, I finally reached a point where it seemed that I had failed in my search. (Of course, I know now that I was not really searching for God, but that God was simply insisting upon revealing Itself to be my Entirety.)

However, despite the fact that I had seen and experienced many so-called healings, I had come to the end of the road of duality. Of course, I was not aware of this fact at the moment. All I knew was that the pain, the weakness, and illness still seemed to persist, despite all the Truth I knew. Again and again, I questioned, "With all the Truth I know, how can this be happening to me?"

Suddenly one day, I found myself wondering whether the Truth I knew was really true or not. Even so, I knew that if I was mistaken, and if I had been deceiving myself, I did not want to go on living. In other words, if the Truth, God, was a myth, there was no hope and no purpose in living at all. Incidentally, I now know that I was filled with self-pity and a certain amount of self-righteousness.

Suddenly an event took place which compelled me to ask: "Just what *do* I know?" I was faced with the fact that the only thing I *really* knew, beyond any doubt, was that I existed. Despite all the years of study, prayer, contemplation, etc., the only thing I could say with positive assurance was that I existed. Despite the many apparent proofs that what I knew was true, it was not proving to be true in my experience at the moment, so I could not actually say that I *knew* that which is true. So I merely said, "I know that I exist."

Then the question came: "How do you know that you exist?" The answer to this question was obvious. So I said, "I know I exist because I am conscious." Then the third question came: "As what Consciousness are you conscious?" Instantly I answered, "There is only one Consciousness, and I have to be conscious *as* God-Consciousness." Incidentally, it is in this latter question and its answer that the word *as* became so vitally important in my vocabulary. But to continue, these three questions and the answers to them terminated forever any questioning as to why evil could seem to appear despite all the Truth I knew.

I perceived with great clarity that God really *is* All and that there is nothing in existence that is not God. Although I had believed I knew the Allness that is God, I suddenly realized that I had fluctuated between my knowing of this fact and a questioning about something that was not God. I saw clearly that by this fluctuation I was dividing my attention between God, who does exist, and evil, which does not exist.

This entire revelation took place during one afternoon, and needless to say, I arose from that chair completely aware of being the Perfection I had always been. Furthermore, the *evidence* of the Truth I now actually *knew* was apparent, and there was no evidence of the nothing called evil to be seen or experienced. Gladly I share this precious experience with you, knowing that it will help you to realize the nothingness of nothing.

Someone has said that when we can look into the face of the devil and see God, we have really found God. This is a very good statement for us to consider. No matter how bad an appearance may be, let us go right on seeing God and God *only*. No matter how persistent it may seem to be, let us refuse to be diverted from our conviction of the fact that God is all that is present. Let us not honor "nothing" by questioning why it *seems* to be "something." Let us not maintain or sustain its appearances by acknowledging its spurious presence and appearance.

Let us honor God and God alone. Let us accept and acknowledge God and God alone. Let us be forever through with questioning why nothing can seem to be something. It can't, you know. And when we know that even the mind that questions is nothing, the questions will naturally cease. You see, Mind knows only Itself. It knows nothing other than Itself about which to question. So any question about evil, nothing, must be asked by non-mind, or a kind of mind that does not exist. It is not surprising that such questions are never satisfactorily answered.

We have stated that there are three ways of questioning and that two of these ways are futile. We have discussed the futility of these ways. So now let us discuss the type of questioning that is right and that is worthwhile. Indeed, the right way of questioning can be gloriously rewarding. In this right way of questioning, the questions are always about the Something that does exist. This "Something" is God. We are well aware of the fact that God is our own Consciousness, so we know that the answer to every right question exists within and as our own God-Consciousness.

Anyone who knows that which is true can write or speak that which is true. However, no one can know that which is true except the knower. This knower is you. In order to fully know that anything is true, you must know why it is true, and the *why* of your awareness must take place as an activity of your own God-Consciousness. All of the written and spoken words in the English language will not make the "why" apparent *to* you. The "why" has to be apparent *as* you. That is, the "why" must appear within and as your own Consciousness.

All right questioning is Self-questioning. There is no God outside for you to question or to whom you can direct questions. You are asking of your God-Self every question pertaining to God. Furthermore, you are asking the question about your Self. Now, if the one who asks the questions and the one who answers are the same One, the question and the answer are the same thing. Thus, the question disappears in the presence of the answer.

As stated before, the answer to every right question anyone could ask exists inherently within and as his own God-Consciousness. Consequently, the answer to the question existed even as the question was being asked. So it is apparent that the question of itself is nothing. It is the answer that brings forth the question and not the question that reveals the answer. Actually, what appeared to be the question was your own Consciousness revealing some specific Truth to Itself, *as* Itself.

The answer to every right question is always established in the basic premise of all Existence. This is the unqualified fact that God is All, All is God. For instance, suppose you were to ask, "Why am I alive?" The answer to this question is that God is Life, God is All; thus, God must be alive as your Life. Life must live in order to be alive, and Life must live in order to be Life. There can be no dead or nonexistent Life. So you are alive because God, the *only* Life, must be alive as your Life.

You can follow this premise through in any right questioning, and you will discover that invariably it will lead you right straight to the Allness, the Onliness, that is God. Thus, finally, the questions no longer appear. Rather, you find your Self constantly listening for your own God-Consciousness to announce the answers that should be revealed at any given moment. Oh, it is truly a free and glorious Life when we just remain as full open Consciousness, constantly listening for, and hearing, the silent Voice of our own God-Consciousness. This, beloved, is our immunity to all false questioning.

"Owe No Man Anything"

In the world of appearance, debt seems to be the order of the day. This situation holds true on the international scene, in the affairs of our Nation; it is true of almost all the business transactions and is true in the experience of most individuals. Just as many nations are burdened by debt, so it is that our Nation and most of our citizens are also burdened by debt. Of course, all of this is in the fallacious world of appearance, but so long as it continues to victimize so many of us, some clarification of this delusion is in order.

Paul well knew the fallacy of debt:

> Owe no man anything, but to love one another: for he that loveth another hath fulfilled the law (Rom. 13:8).

Just prior to this statement, Paul had adjured his hearers:

> Render therefore to all their dues: tribute to whom tribute is due; custom to whom custom; fear to whom fear; honor to whom honor (Rom. 13:7).

From these statements, it is obvious Paul was clearly aware that there seem to be many aspects of indebtedness. If there were anything genuine about indebtedness, this would be true. However, there *is* the necessity to "owe no man anything."

Perhaps one of the worst aspects of the feeling of indebtedness is that it tends to rob one of his feeling of freedom and joy. Anything that appears to be burdensome is also binding and limiting. Wherever there appears to be one that is obligated, there appears to be one in debt.

So-called human obligations are always burdensome. This is true in every phase of our daily living. For instance, have you ever felt that you must invite certain friends to dinner because they had previously entertained you at dinner? Of course, this is a very small example, but it portrays in a simple and homely way the false sense of obligation that accompanies indebtedness. Of course, if you invite these friends to dinner not because you feel obligated to them, but rather, through a sincere, loving sense of wanting them to come, this is the normal and natural way in which to "render custom to whom custom" is due. If all our social affairs were conducted in this way, they would always be joyous and free occasions. It is in this way that "he that loveth another hath fulfilled the law."

To owe no man anything means to be free of all false sense of burdensome human obligations. This does not mean that one should not "render therefore to all their dues." Rather, it means that every so-called debt should be paid, and be paid promptly, when it is due. However, if the debt is paid with a false sense of strain and a burdensome sense of compulsion, the Love that is inherent in and *as* your Consciousness is not fulfilling its purpose.

Now, we have discussed this aspect of daily living as though it were actually genuine, and we know the entire human scene is but an illusory concept *about* the glorious, free, joyous Existence which is genuine. However, every normal and good so-called human activity is an indication of some actual, spiritual, omniactive fact. Our necessity is to look *beyond* the seeming human activity and discern the genuine, spiritual, omniactive *fact* that is being evidenced as what appears to be a human activity.

The basic omniactive fact is that all activity is God in action. As you know, God is one infinite, eternal, indivisible, omniactive Essence. Consequently, there can actually be no such thing as debt *and* debtor. Paul was right in saying, "Owe no man anything." Is the Mind that is God in debt to Itself? Does Consciousness burden Itself? Does Love obligate Itself to Itself? Does infinite Intelligence borrow from Itself? Does infinite God lack any of Its Completeness?

Within the answers to these questions, you will discover that basically all so-called borrowing and lending is wrong. By this same token, all installment buying is wrong. Now, let us see just why these practices, so largely accepted today, are not based in Truth.

All borrowing and all credit buying is based on the fallacious illusion that there is a present lack of supply. This goes right back to the further illusion that Supply is divisible and that one specific Identity has more of Supply than has the one who borrows or who buys on credit. But this is not all. All borrowing or credit is based on the fallacy that Supply is not present in and as Completeness right here and now. The assumption is that right now the supply is absent, but at some future date it will be present.

Whenever we say, "I don't have the money for something or some activity right now, but I will have it later," we have denied the Presence of infinite, indivisible Supply right now. We have also falsely stated that right now we are incomplete but that later we hope to be complete. Just so long as we continue to look to the so-called future for our Supply, it will seem always to be in the future. So long as this fallacy continues, we will never seem to have quite enough supply present right here and right now. We cannot deny the presence of indivisible Supply and expect to see the evidence of Supply present right here and right now.

There is just as much of Supply present now as there will ever be. Furthermore, there is just as complete Supply present now as there has ever been. There is no time in which Supply can be present other than now. *There is no time*. Thus, there is no future in which more of Supply is going to appear. Neither is there a past in which Supply has been lost or has disappeared. Can God be absent from Itself?

Now of course, in the assumptive human scene, nations are going to go right on borrowing from each other. Our Nation is going to continue to function on borrowed money; our businesses and corporations are going to continue to operate in this same way; our citizens will keep right on buying on the installment plan. All of this will continue until the assumptive human mind is perceived to be nothing —no mind at all. You see, this illusory mind is never satisfied. Always it yearns for something it does not have. It may yearn for power; its unsatisfied longing may be for great wealth; or it may be just a desire to satisfy so-called human pride or vanity.

It is always the assumptive mind of man that yearns for the things of the world. It will plunge itself head over heels into debt in order to satisfy this yearning. It is always seeking satisfaction in one way or another. It cannot act intelligently because it is not intelligent. It is not Mind—Intelligence in action.

Jesus well knew the fallacy of any attempt to satisfy human longing for wealth, prestige, or power. He knew the "things of this world" could never satisfy the voracious, non-intelligent, human mind. It is interesting to note that the very last temptation in the wilderness was an offer of all the wealth and all the power of the world:

> Again, the devil taketh him up into an exceeding high mountain, and showeth him all the kingdoms of the world, and the glory of them; And saith unto him, All these things will I give thee, if thou wilt fall down and worship me.
>
> Then saith Jesus unto him, Get thee hence, Satan: for it is written, Thou shalt worship the Lord thy God, and him only shalt thou serve. Then the devil leaveth him, and, behold, angels came and ministered unto him (Matt. 4:8-11).

Of course, this episode is couched in terms that seem very orthodox. But there are several profound spiritual Truths to be realized in an enlightened contemplation of this recorded event. In fact, a deep contemplation of this entire record of the temptations will be very rewarding to students of the Ultimate. But for our purpose right now, it is sufficient to recognize the spiritually significant facts portrayed in the above quotations.

For instance, Jesus must have been faced with the possibility that he could claim great power, wealth, and prestige if he would only let the little personal "I" claim something of itself. This is the basic argument of illusion. It is well to note that Jesus had to go *all the way* in his rejection of the little "I." He had to perceive that "man with breath in his nostrils" could possess nothing because this assumptive identity *was* nothing. Jesus well knew that to claim possessions is to become a slave to that which he is to possess supposedly. He knew that even if he could possess all the kingdoms of the world and he rendered all the glory of mankind, it really meant nothing because it was all illusion.

You will note that he said, "Thou shalt worship the Lord thy God, and him only shalt thou serve" (Matt. 4:10).

Well, who is "the Lord thy God" other than your own Consciousness? Whom can we serve, honor, other than this same God-Consciousness? An awareness of the fact that God is the *only* Mind of any one of us means that we yearn for nothing of this world. Rather, we know that within and as our Consciousness exists the infinite, indivisible completeness which constitutes all Supply.

Right about now, you may be asking some questions, such as, "But what about the money I owe right now? What about my inability to pay my present debts?" Well, you have just been reading some basic Truths pertaining to Supply. Right now, every Truth is true. Right now, every Truth is present. Right now, you are conscious. Thus, right now, you are conscious of the Truth that Supply is present within and *as* your own Consciousness. The awareness of Supply and the evidence of Supply are inseparable because the evidence and the Consciousness of Truth are the very same Essence.

The seeming indebtedness is not what it appears to be in your experience. The fact that you are reading this article indicates that you are ready to realize the indivisible nature of Supply. This is your own Consciousness being enlightened. In fact, this is the Supply that already exists *as* your own Consciousness, revealing and evidencing Itself *as* your Consciousness. At this point, it would be well for you to return to an issue of *The Word* in which an article entitled "Supply" was presented. This article was revealed in *The Word* you received in April 1961. If you will reread and contemplate this article now, you will realize much more of its great spiritual significance than was apparent when you first read it.

The so-called debt is unnatural, and this is why it has seemed to be burdensome. Whenever we seem to depart from Absolute Truth in any way, we also seem to be in difficulty. However, the fact remains: Supply *is* present, and It is inexhaustible, so the seeming debt can be paid. However, there are some Truths it would be well to consider, even though you are apparently paying a so-called human debt.

For instance, it is well to realize that Love is fulfilling Its own activity. Consequently, you will not pay any so-called debt grudgingly or through any false sense of burdensome obligation. You will not pay it for any selfish purpose, such as an effort to maintain your credit or even to relieve yourself from embarrassment. Rather, you will recognize that this activity is Love in action; thus, it is completely free from any seeming selfish motive. You will act in the way that is necessary at the moment because you are functioning as the Principle which is Love Itself. No matter how burdensome the fallacious debt may seem to be, you will joyously and lovingly function as the Principle which is Love in this experience.

Oh, Truth is so simple and uncomplicated. It is only in the illusory human picture that everything seems so complicated. If we are to realize the beautiful simplicity of the Truth that *is* All, it is necessary to constantly stay with the basic fact that *God is All* in every experience.

Questions and Answers

Q: If everything in existence is eternal, how can you account for the disappearance of all the beautiful trees that are being destroyed in the name of progress? For instance, much of our most beautiful scenery is being destroyed by superhighways, housing projects, and other manmade works.

A: If we accept the fact that God is All, All is God, we cannot accept the illusion that any Substance is subject to destruction. Neither can we accept the fallacy that a destructive mind or power exists. Either God is All or God is not All. If God is All—and this is Truth—then every aspect of God is an eternal Existent. An eternal Existent can have no beginning; neither can it have an ending. God is the Substance of all Existence. Thus, all Substance is beginningless, changeless, and endless.

The assumptive mind of man clings tenaciously to the illusion of birth, beginning. By this same token, this same non-intelligence must also accept death, an ending. Everything in the illusory realm of the so-called material world is temporal. It has to be thus because the very basis of its pretended existence is temporal. The "things" of this world that *appear* to be comprised of density, matter, can only appear to be seen by the temporal eyes and known by the temporal mind of an illusory, temporal man.

God, being the *only* Substance, is the only Substance that can actually be seen as eternal and imperishable. Furthermore, God is the only Vision that can see, and the Vision that is God can only see Itself. There really is no difference between the seer and that which is seen. In our book *The Ultimate*, there is a chapter entitled "Seeing Is Being." A clear perception of the Truths stated in that chapter will reveal the indestructible nature of All that is ever seen or known.

The Vision that is God seeing sees only eternal, uninterrupted Perfection. The fallacious vision that is called man seeing sees only its own imperfect, temporal delusions. But the Vision that is God is genuine and does exist. The illusory vision of assumptive man is fallacious and does not actually exist. The Vision that is God, aware of Itself, sees all that exists. Needless to say, this Vision does not see anything that is imperfect or subject to destruction. The Vision that is God seeing is the enlightened Consciousness of you, of me, and of every genuine Identity.

As enlightened Consciousness, we see spiritually. Thus, we speak of spiritual Vision. This clear, spiritual Vision is unimpeded by any false covering, the veil, called eyes of matter. Spiritual Vision sees the things of Spirit. Spiritual Vision is the only vision, so there is nothing existing that can be seen other than the things of Spirit.

Enlightened Consciousness sees things as they are. This infinite Vision is limitless, and thus, it sees an infinite variety of Beauty. It sees Beauty that is unimaginable by the assumptive mind of man. It sees only that which is here to see, and It sees only the eternal, uninterrupted Perfection of Its own immutable Nature. Spiritual Vision *is* enlightened Consciousness, and this eternal, perfect Vision is aware *only* of Its own beginningless, changeless, endless Essence. Therefore It is aware of nothing that is destructible. Neither is It aware of a destructive illusion called the mind of man.

Why

I gaze into the peaceful sky,
And as I contemplate the "why"
Of seeming turmoil pain,
I realize, as sudden Light
Reveals no pain, no turmoil, blight,
Can be, and it is vain
To question that which only *seems*
To be in man's illusory dreams.

Thus heaven and earth are known to be
Inseparably One, and I can see
That living Love is Life;
And futile questions but obscure
The Vision Infinite so pure,
So free from trouble, strife;
The all-revealing Light hath shown,
Perfection is. None else is known.

Light and Love
Marie S. Watts

November 1963

In the beginning was the Word, and the Word was with God, and the Word was God.

—John 1:1

Dear One,

I must share with you one of the most joyous aspects of our classes and lectures. Always, when I return for the classes and lectures, it is such great joy to see the greater light and joy in your faces. But this is not all; the Truths you have been experiencing are evident as every aspect of your beings and bodies.

The world would say that you look younger and more healthy. It would even say that your movements are more free and younger But we know this is not true. We know that always you remain at the very zenith of Perfection. And we know that all that has taken place is your greater awareness of the eternal Perfection you are, have always been, and will always be.

In any event, my joy is indescribable in seeing this evidence of your greater awareness of what you are. This is but one wonderful aspect of our study and contemplation of the Ultimate. Not only do the illusory lines of strain and struggle disappear from your faces, the Light that you *are* shines and is evident as the very expression of your faces. The Light you *are* is more apparent. It shines. And it is all God revealing Itself as your ever greater awareness of Being. It is God, increasingly *revealing Itself to be all there is of your Self.*

We know that no so-called human pride or ego can enter into any revelation of the Ultimate. If for one moment any little assumptive human attempted to claim credit for

God's revelations of Himself, all revelation would cease. This is true because any false sense of human ego is darkness, and it would surely seem to obscure the Light if it were to become swollen with its own false sense, delusions of grandeur, of its own importance. Thus, we stand in complete humility, in awe, and we marvel that God should so gloriously reveal His Allness, His Onliness.

Again we find that the Thanksgiving season is with us. No doubt you will reread the November issues of *The Word* for 1961 and 1962. However, revelation is a constant experience, and there is a certain spiritual significance pertaining to Thanksgiving. So let us see what God reveals as further enlightenment pertaining to this spiritual significance. I know that the Thanksgiving holiday will be a joyous experience for you. It has to be thus, because you are Joy Itself. But you do not wait until the day named Thanksgiving arrives to recognize and experience *being* the Joy you are.

The Genuine Significance of Thanksgiving

The observance of Thanksgiving Day has many facets. All of us are familiar with the manner in which this holiday is observed. We are also familiar with the fact that sometimes this day is not observed from a religious standpoint, but rather, it is used as an excuse to celebrate in ways that are definitely materialistic.

Of course, we do not observe Thanksgiving Day from an orthodox religious standpoint. Needless to say, we do not celebrate any day from a materialistic standpoint. Yet there is something good, normal, and wonderful about the recognition of Thanksgiving Day, and we cannot, nor do we wish to, criticize or ignore this day which has genuine spiritual significance and which also has definite historical significance.

Before we begin our exploration and consideration of the spiritual significance of Thanksgiving Day, let us be fully aware of the following fact: we do not set aside one day each year and reserve this day for our specific contemplation of the Truths symbolized by Thanksgiving Day. We recognize this day when it occurs; we realize its genuine continuance of our contemplation throughout the year. Whatever is good and normal in *any* day focuses our attention upon the spiritual significance of whatever Truth is being symbolized. In fact, every day is filled with seemingly human happenings that are simply symbolic of genuine spiritual facts. Let us consider a very simple illustration of this fact.

Our first greeting in the morning starts with the word *good!* "Good morning" is the usual greeting of friends and families. This is symbolic, but behind the symbol there is a spiritual fact. Every morning is a good morning because God is the only Presence of any morning. In fact, God *is* the morning, so it has to be good and perfect. This is genuine fact, symbolized by the simple expression "Good morning."

Likewise, when we start the car and it runs smoothly, transporting us to our employment, it appears that we have simply acted humanly and that the car is strictly a material machine, mechanically perfect enough to run smoothly and fulfill *our* purpose. Ah, but this is only the symbolic appearance. Let us consider just a very few spiritual facts behind this symbology. Of course, the symbol is nothing of itself. Yet the spiritual fact symbolized is important, and it is genuine.

This is a smooth, successful, orderly, active Universe. Therefore, your activity, the activity of your car, the activity of your entire affairs is a smooth, successful, orderly activity. Furthermore, this same orderly activity is the *only* activity of your *only* Body. Every good, joyous, and perfect experience you have in your daily affairs is really good, perfect, and joyous because God, the All, is Goodness, Perfection, Joy. These joyous experiences may appear to be merely human experiences. But actually there are no human experiences. There is only One who can experience, and this One is God. The experience *is* the Experiencer, and the Experiencer is the experience.

We cannot ignore these good experiences, even though they may appear to be misinterpreted and considered to be human experiences. Every normal, good, joyous, free activity is a God-experience. In fact, it is God experiencing *being* Itself. It is true that these wonderful activities *appear* to be human experiences. But they are not what they appear to be. Present in and *as* every joyous, perfect, and satisfying activity, there is the joy, the Perfection, the Completeness that is God in action—omnipresent Omniaction.

We must see *beyond* the human misinterpretation of any good and normal experience. We must acknowledge and perceive the genuine spiritual experience which is being symbolized by, or appears to be, a human experience. In other words, we "judge not by appearance," but we perceive and judge according to the spiritual significance behind any good, normal, and perfect experience.

It is in this same way that we read, study, and contemplate our Bible. If we were to misinterpret these wonderful Truths we read, we would certainly misunderstand God. To misunderstand God would be to misunderstand our own God-Identity. We know that our Bible is replete with glorious statements of Absolute Truth. Yet the generally accepted orthodox interpretations of these statements present a false picture of duality. Even some of the statements attributed to Jesus the Christ appear to be decidedly dualistic. Yet spiritual perception of the genuine spiritual significance of these statements reveals the Oneness, the Allness, the Onliness which is God. Thus, we are not deceived by the words. Rather, we are enlightened by the Word Itself, and the Word is our own God-Consciousness.

Now we are ready to explore some of the deeper, more profound Truths pertaining to Thanksgiving Day. We are familiar with the historical aspect of this holiday. We know that the Pilgrims set aside this one day in order that they might give thanks for protection and for survival. Also they met on this day to give thanks for crops, food, and for every good experience they had encountered during what had appeared to be a very trying and difficult human experience.

Now, these pioneers could have credited themselves only for any good that had been experienced or accomplished. But the wonderful aspect of their decision to observe a day of thanks is that they were not claiming human credit or glory, as though they had accomplished some great thing by sheer human effort. It is true that they no doubt believed their good had been accomplished with the help of God. Nonetheless, the fundamental Truth back of all of this is the submergence of the assumptive little "I" in the recognition of the necessity for the presence of God. Therefore, the spiritual significance of this first Thanksgiving meeting is the fact that the presence of the God *I* was recognized, accepted, and credited with being Good.

Needless to say, the Consciousness of the Pilgrims had to be the presence of the God-Consciousness in order to recognize God in or as their affairs at all. It takes the Mind that *is* God to be aware of God. It takes the Consciousness that *is* God to be aware of God. It takes the Presence of God to be aware of the Presence of God. Consequently, the observance of the first Thanksgiving Day signifies the Presence that is God, or Good. This is the genuine spiritual significance of the first observance of Thanksgiving Day.

The Pilgrims who first observed Thanksgiving Day were not glorifying themselves as nonexistent human beings. Rather, they were giving full credit where credit belongs —to God. It is true that their seeming mistake was in the orthodox illusion that God was a Being separate from, or other than, themselves But at least they were not feeding the little assumptive ego in their observance of that first Thanksgiving Day. Any occasion that dispels, even temporarily, the illusory self-important "I" is good and is fraught with spiritual significance. You see, it is this illusory little selfish "I" that is the basis of all dualism.

Now let us perceive more of the basic aspects signifying the presence of God in the observance of Thanksgiving Day. There can be no doubt but that the first Thanksgiving Day was a day of joyous festivities, a day of rejoicing. Well, Joy is a universal, omnipresent Truth. Thus, Joy is natural and normal. Our Bible is abundantly sprinkled with exhortations to rejoice. The joyous experience of Being is a spiritual experience. It may appear to be a human experience, but actually it is spiritual in its entire Nature. Actually, Joy is one of the most important aspects of Thanksgiving Day.

Of course, we do not give thanks to a God whom we consider to be separate from, or other than, our own God-Identity. The genuine spiritual meaning of Thanksgiving is Joy. God *is* Joy. Thus, God is a joyous God. To rejoice is to experience *being* the presence of Joy, and this is a spiritual experience.

Gratitude, rightly interpreted, means Joy. It also means Love. It has been said that the Pilgrims invited the Indians to the first Thanksgiving festivities and observance. It is also said that the Indians brought food, maize, and wild turkeys to the feast. Right here in this incident, we have an example of Oneness, and Oneness is Love.

Oh, there are so many aspects of the spiritual significance of just this one holiday. For instance, although the Pilgrims had seemed to suffer great hardship, hunger, and lack the preceding winter, the summer had produced a good crop, and the harvest was bounteous. There can be no doubt but that the seeming lack and the hardships were obliterated in the joyous observance of the first Thanksgiving Day. It was not the former seeming lack they were considering. Rather, it was the *abundance* that was present right then and there that made them rejoice.

Here again, we can perceive a spiritual Fact of great significance. *The abundance is omnipresent.* Abundance has to be ever-present because there is never a lack of God. Furthermore, there is never a dearth of God being conscious. Consciousness is *always* conscious, and It is always conscious of what It *is*. The very Substance and activity of Abundance is God-Consciousness. Consequently, abundant Consciousness signifies complete abundance in every aspect of daily living.

When the Pilgrims rejoiced because their crops were so abundant, the very presence of God *as* abundant food was being signified. Even though they did not perceive this profound spiritual significance, its Truth was true all the while. And this same Truth is true right here and right now.

Herein we have focused our attention upon just a very few of the innumerable aspects of God which are revealed so clearly in the observance of Thanksgiving. Day. We would be much enlightened and inspired if we were to contemplate many more of the aspects of this occasion. But we will experience much greater enlightenment if we continue this contemplation throughout *every* occasion of *every* day. Our days are God-filled days. Indeed, this is true because there is nothing other than God to *be* the day or the night.

Let us be quick to perceive the genuine God-significance of each and every joyous, good, perfect, and normal event in our daily experience. In this way, we will not be accepting duality. We will not be considering the so-called human experience to be one aspect of existence and the spiritual experience to be another aspect of Being. Rather, we will realize that the omnipotent Omnipresence that is God is the *only* Experience and the *only* Experiencer. We will also perceive that every good and perfect Experience, even though it *appears* to be a human event, is actually a spiritual Experience. It can be no other because it is all God, experiencing being Its joyous, eternal, perfect Self.

The Gift of God

> And seek not ye what ye shall eat, or what ye shall drink, neither be ye of doubtful mind. For all these things do the nations of the world seek after: and your Father knoweth that ye have need of these things.
>
> But rather seek ye the kingdom of God; and all these things shall be added unto you. Fear not, little flock; for it is your Father's good pleasure: to give you the kingdom (Luke 12: 29-32).

The foregoing statements from our Bible are so fraught with spiritual significance that an entire book could be written using just these statements as its basis. Let us consider just a few of the more outstanding Truths portrayed in these verses. All of us have read orthodox interpretations of these statements; all of us have read or heard them interpreted from a metaphysical standpoint. However, there is a far deeper meaning presented in these words of Jesus than any orthodox or metaphysical interpretation has presented.

Just before Jesus made the foregoing statements to the multitude, he mentioned the lilies, pointing out some salient facts. He clearly revealed the basic Truth that the lilies fulfilled their purpose not by doing, but by *being*. He did not mean that the lilies were inactive. He did mean that the activity of the lilies was the omniactive Presence, just *being*. The activity of being is altogether different from the activity of doing. As Jesus points out, the activity of being is completely free from effort, strain, or struggle. It is necessary to perceive this significant Truth if we are to be completely free from doubt or fear.

The Beauty and the glory of the lilies is God *being*. The activity of God being is not God's gift *to* the lilies. Rather, it is God's pleasure in *being* the lilies. It is God being Itself, of course. Yet it is the Life, the Beauty, the Substance that is God, being that specific aspect of Itself. This explains why it is not necessary for the lily to struggle to do something or to be something of itself. It simply *is*, and it has no choice other than to *be what it is*. When we fully perceive this Truth, we can no longer be of "doubtful mind."

For years we have said, "The gift of God is Himself." You will find this statement in some of the earlier writings of the Ultimate. Whether or not you have ever read or made this statement of Truth, you have always known it to be true. This Truth has always been present in and as your Consciousness. The gift of God is God being Itself. The gift of God is not God's gift *to* you; rather, it is God *being* You. Although it is God being God, it is God being Itself as the specific aspect of Itself which constitutes all there is of You.

The gift of God is God being the Mind that knows nothing of doubt or fear. This Mind, actively *being* Itself, is your Mind. Consequently, the Mind you have, and *are*, is completely free from doubt or fear. There is no uncertainty in and as the Mind that is God. There is no uncertainty in and as the Mind that is God being You. Mind is no less Mind, Intelligence is no less Intelligence, whether It is manifested as that aspect of Itself called You or whether It is evident as the Universal Intelligence. The Mind that knows Itself to *be* All Existence is not concerned with getting, attaining, or obtaining anything.

Therefore, we do not seek, we do not struggle, for the "things of the world." We are not concerned with getting, attaining, or obtaining anything. Our first, last, and *only* interest is the realization of the kingdom of God.

The kingdom is the Consciousness which is God. The Consciousness which is God is aware of *being* All; thus, It is aware of being complete. There can be no awareness of incompleteness, for there is no consciousness that is aware of being incomplete. If anything necessary to your completeness could be missing, God, Consciousness, would have to be conscious of being incomplete. The gift of God is the kingdom, Consciousness, which you are, actively aware of *being* complete.

It is impossible to reconcile the Mind that knows Itself to be All with an assumptive mind that is concerned with attaining or obtaining anything. The Mind that *is* All is irreconcilable with an assumptive mind that is not aware of being *anything*. The gift of God is the presence of your awareness of *being* all that is essential to your complete, free, joyous existence.

The gift of God is All that God is. God is eternal Life, and the Presence, gift, of Life is your *eternal* Life. God is infinite, eternal, uninterrupted Consciousness, and the Presence of this Consciousness is your Consciousness. God is infinite, eternal Mind, Intelligence, and the Presence, gift, of this Intelligence is your Mind. God is infinite, immutable, eternal Love, and the Presence, gift, of this Love is your Love. God is uninterrupted Perfection. Thus, the Presence of uninterrupted Perfection is your Perfection, right here and right now. It is because the gift of God is Himself that you are joyous, free, unlimited, boundless, and forever complete. You see, the Presence of Completeness is complete.

As you can see, the gift of God is the presence of God. But it is well to realize that the gift of God is the *complete* presence of God. This means that God is present in and as your entire Existence, your Life, your home, profession, business, your entire Being, and of course, your Body.

We have said that God is the only Substance, and this is true. To some of you, the word *Essence* better expresses what you feel God to be *as* Substance. It is always well to use whatever word feels right to you. The Essence, Substance, of God *is* God. The Substance of Spirit *is* Spirit, and Spirit is Consciousness.

As you know, Consciousness is Awareness of Being. It follows, then, that Awareness of Being really is Substance, the Substance which is God. The gift of God is God being the Awareness of Being, which is the Substance, Essence, of your Body. This is not all. This Awareness of Being is the Essence of everything and everyone who exists in and as your universe. As we have often stated, "Your Consciousness is your Universe." If you perceive this Truth with clarity, you will realize how impossible it is for the Substance of your Body to be imperfect. You will also realize the impossibility of *any* imperfect Body, Substance, having existence. Indeed, your Universe is a pleasant Universe because it is a perfect Universe.

There is another aspect of the gift of God that is of primary importance. The perfect activity of the Essence which is God must be clearly perceived. The gift of God is Its omniactive Essence. But because God is Intelligence, this omniactive Essence has to be intelligently active. Thus, this activity has to be perfect activity. You know that the gift of God is the Presence of God, being You.

Now, it is well to realize that the Presence of God, being You, is the Presence of perfect Omniaction as *your* activity. This means that the activity of your daily affairs, your business, profession, and your home is perfect activity. Furthermore, it means that the activity of the entire Essence of your Body is perfect activity. In this perception, you will realize the Presence of the perfect Essence in constant, uninterrupted, perfect action. In all our seeing, it is well to perceive the omnipresence of perfect, conscious Omniaction.

> It is your Father's good pleasure to give you the kingdom (Luke 12:32).

This is a very important statement. As we have stated, the word *kingdom* really means *Consciousness*. The Consciousness, the Awareness, of these Truths is of vital importance for all of us. No matter how true any Truth may be, or is, it will not seem to be apparent as your experience unless you are *aware*, conscious, of this Truth. To be fully aware of any Truth is to be conscious of *being* this Truth. So the greatest gift of all is the Presence of the Consciousness, the Awareness, of the Truth you are and know your Self to be.

It is God's good pleasure to be present as your Life. It is God's good pleasure to be present as your Intelligence and as your Intelligence in action. It is God's good pleasure to be present as the Love you are. Really, *you* are the presence of God's good and perfect pleasure. This is the gift of God *being* your entire Life, Activity, Mind, Love, and above all, your Consciousness. Consider these Truths, for they are true right here and right now. They are true *as you* because you *are* the Truth which has always been and will ever be complete, free, perfect, and eternal.

Just recently, we received a communication entitled "My Tribute to *The Word*." It reveals such great enlightenment and Beauty that we feel impelled to share it with you. Therefore, instead of the question and the usual poem at the close of *The Word*, we have included this illumined one's glorious perception of God, appearing as *The Word.*

A Tribute to *The Word*

What is there about *The Word* that I love so much? Is it because of the beautiful words it contains? Why, oh why, does it have such an appeal to me.

The minute I take *The Word* out of the envelope, here before opening to the first page, the cover reminds me that the Consciousness I am is the Universe I am. [The original cover for *The Word* included the letter "U," symbolizing the Universe—Ed.] Then I am the activity that is everywhere present. God is the Self that I am, and there can be no Selfhood apart from the One. *The Word* is the one revealing itself *as the Self that I Am, as the Self that You are, as the Self of Everyone who exists in the Universe.*

The Word reveals the boundless activity that is everywhere present, and I am that activity. There is no place where this activity begins, no place where it ends. It is Omniaction. I am reminded of the Love that I am, the Mind that I am, the Consciousness that I am, the Life that I am.

Oh, *The Word* is not a periodical in the ordinary sense of the word. It is God revealing the Self that I am. Its so-called printed pages remind me of the *I* that I am. It reveals I am not one *with* God, for *I* am not an Identity apart, or other than, God identifying Itself *as* me, as you, as everyone. We are of one household, one Consciousness. No longer a feeling of separateness but rather, the One Being the One that You are, specifically identified. Here there is one Body, not bodies many. Here is one Identity, not identities many.

It is well to pause to be fully aware of what *The Word* is. It is not just so many sheets of printed paper. Oh no, never! It reminds me that where *I* am, ye are also. Oh, but wait until you begin turning the pages and the Light you are is revealed! Yes, the Light in which there is no darkness at all. Then the awareness of Oneness, not separateness; the awareness of Love, not hate; the awareness of Life, not death; the awareness of Intelligence, not ignorance; the awareness of Self-completeness, Self-perfection, and above all, the awareness that this Self-completeness, Self-perfection, is just what I am—it is God, revealing Himself to be the Self that I am.

While illusions would have me believe in that which I am not, *The Word* reveals the Light that *I* am. When *The Word* is read for the first time, there is a feeling of fullness; then, as it is reread again and again, there is no longer a reason to read anymore, but just let the Light that I am *be* the Self that I am. Then I not only walk in the Light, but I am aware of being the Light that *I* am—am walking in. Then there is the awareness of being in the world but not of it. It is like looking into a mirror and realizing that what you see *is not you*.

The Word reveals the Love that I am. Is it not because of the Love that I am that *The Word* reveals the Love that *I* am? Is not *The Word* but the Self, revealing the Love that never was born, that never changes, that never dies? As the Consciousness that I am is the Love that *I* am, is not this Love that *I* am conscious of being evident everywhere?

Whereas I seemingly toiled and labored to be, now I am the Activity that is laborless, toilless. No longer seeking to be, but knowing what I am and being what I know.

The Word knows it is Something. That Something is You, is Me, is Everyone; that Something is God evidencing Itself. Consciousness and evidence are inseparable. This is what *The Word* means to me, and much more, for pages could not contain nor books hold all *The Word* reveals. But be patient in your contemplations, and *The Word* will do the rest. It is a Pearl of great price. No price can be put upon it, for its value can only be revealed as you contemplate the Truth it states. *The Word* is You, *God identified*, the Christ.

Light and Love,
Marie S. Watts

December 1963

In the beginning was the Word, and the Word was with God, and the Word was God.

—John 1:1

Dear One,

I have mentioned this before, but as it is becoming increasingly apparent, I feel it is worth mentioning again. Students of the Ultimate are obviously *evidencing* the Truth they are perceiving. The seeming appearance of worry and strain is erased, and the faces are alight with great joy and peace. Furthermore, every one of them shows forth a greater sense of youth, freshness, newness, and just glowing health. Needless to say, my Joy is boundless when I perceive these manifestations of the Truths we know to be true.

One of the most satisfying aspects of our activity is the realization that our revelations during any class, seminar, or even private contemplation are not limited by any boundaries of any kind. We are aware that our Consciousness is boundless. We are also aware that the Consciousness of everyone is boundless. Thus, we know that anyone who is ready to perceive any specific Truth we are knowing may also perceive this same Truth.

This is unselfed Love in action. This is the way in which the world must be enlightened. Above all, this is the way it is taking place. It is a glorious experience to realize that every silent contemplation is going on not only as the Consciousness of the Identity who is contemplating but also as the world Consciousness. It has to be this way because the Consciousness of the Identity *is* the world Consciousness and the Universal Consciousness.

Many of you tell us that you now know the true meaning of illumination. But better still, you now know that you have experienced this glorious enlightenment many times but did not recognize it to be illumination. One of your precious letters says, "No longer do I feel unworthy to experience illumination. Neither do I feel unprepared. I never dreamed it could be like this."

Your letters reveal one incontrovertible fact: *no longer do you deny your illumined Consciousness.* Thus, you do not limit the *boundless* scope of your already illumined Consciousness. It truly is glorious to perceive the sudden loosening of the seemingly self-forged chains of limitation.

How wonderful it is to realize that when we speak of God, we are really speaking of your entire Being, of my entire Being, and of the entire Being of every Identity in existence. You see, it is *your* God-Consciousness that is revealing these glorious Truths. It is also my God-Consciousness. Actually, it is the God-Consciousness which is conscious as everyone. Even though there may not appear to be many who realize this basic Truth, the fact remains: *the universal Consciousness is God being conscious.*

Shortly after you receive this issue of *The Word*, the world will be celebrating what is generally believed to be the birth of Christ. Although we know that the Christ was never born, we also recognize the fact that there is much that is good about the Christmas season. For instance, in the unselfed giving at Christmas time, there is not very much of the assumptive little "I" in evidence. There is unselfed Love evidenced on every side. All of this is good. Any event that draws our attention away from the selfish, deluded little "I" is good. Therefore, we welcome and enjoy this season of the year.

Those of us who are really aware of the Nature of the Christ are glad to be reminded of the birthless, deathless Christ-Consciousness. We rejoice in the awareness that the illumined Christ-Consciousness is the genuine and *only* Consciousness of each one of us. Furthermore, we rejoice in the Joy that is apparent as those who do not yet *seem* to be aware that they too are the illumined Christ-Consciousness.

The Truths revealed in our new book, *You Are the Splendor,* will give this Christmas season a deeper meaning than ever before. No doubt many of you will refer to former articles in *The Word* that pertain to Christmas. Needless to say, you will discover deeper and more glorious Truths now, as you read and contemplate these articles. Of course, the most wonderful aspect of these revelations is the fact that every Truth that is revealed *to* you has always existed *as* you, as your own God-Consciousness. Herein is your complete freedom from the fallacy of leader, teacher, system, or organization.

The Eternal Christ

At this season of the year, it is well to consider the eternal Nature of the Christ. On every side, we hear about the birth of Jesus the Christ. Then, during the Easter season, we hear about the death of this same Jesus the Christ. If the Christ could be born, death would be inevitable because a beginning always signifies an ending. But the Christ is eternal; thus, the Christ was never born, nor can there be death in or as the eternal Nature of the Christ. It is true that Easter Sunday is supposed to signify the resurrection of the Christ. Yet the inference is that the resurrection followed the death of Jesus the Christ.

The Christ is as eternal as is God because God *is* the Christ. The All-Consciousness that is God evidences Itself as an infinite variety of aspects. Every aspect of the God-Consciousness *is* the God-Consciousness. Every aspect of the God-Consciousness has to be comprised of this God-

Consciousness because there is nothing else for it to be. Thus, the Christ-Consciousness is that aspect of God which we call Man.

You will note the use of the capital *M* in the reference to that aspect of God called Man. If we speak or write of man who is supposedly mortal and temporal, we are not speaking of any aspect of God. Indeed, every aspect of God *is* God Himself, and God certainly is not a mortal being. Neither is God a temporal being. Rather, God is Immortality and Eternality. Thus, every aspect of God has to be immortal and eternal. Man, spelled with a capital *M* is the *only* Man, and this Man is the Christ. Furthermore, Man, the Christ, is God specifically *being* the Christ, or Man. God being Man is distinct from God being Bird, Tree, Planet, or whatever. If God be All, then All is God, and there can be *nothing* existing that is not God *being* That.

That aspect of God called Bird is that specific aspect of God and no other. This is true of any aspect of God, no matter whether we call it Tree, Rose, or Planet. If God were to reveal Himself as but one aspect of His Allness, that specific aspect of God would comprise this entire Universe. For instance, if God were to manifest Himself only as Tree, this Universe would consist of Trees and nothing else. But God's manifestation of His Allness is infinite, innumerable, and infinite in variety. This is the manifested Completeness which is God that constitutes this Universe.

There is one important fact that should be considered right here. *God is indivisible*. The fact that God manifests Itself as an infinite variety of aspects of Itself does not mean that God is separable. The conscious, living, loving Intelligence that is God remains as one indivisible One, no matter how infinite may be the aspects of this One. The indivisibility of God must be realized in the consideration of *any* aspect of God. To consider any aspect of God without realizing the inseparable Nature of God would be to drop back into duality.

The semantics of words can be very misleading. The word *specific* can seem to mean something separate. But our use of this word *specific* has to do with distinction rather than with separateness. For instance, every color in and as the Universe exists in and as each specific color. Yet each color is that distinct color and no other. This gives us a hint of the genuine meaning of this word *specific*.

Speaking of the ways in which words can be misleading, you will note the references to God as Him, He, Himself, as though God were considered to be masculine. Yet we know that gender has nothing to do with God. Really, it makes no difference whether we refer to God as Himself, Herself, or Itself, so long as we are aware that we are referring to the One Infinite All.

Now let us return to our subject, the eternal Christ. We have discussed the fact that the Christ is that specific aspect of God which we have named Man. We realize that God—eternal, conscious, living Mind—could not exist as an aspect of Itself that was temporary. God exists as every aspect of Itself. God does not exist as anything or anyone who appears to begin or to end. Thus, birth and death are but opposite ends of the same illusion. But Man is no illusion. Man exists, and the existence of Man is as eternal as is the Existence of God. It has to be thus because God can only exist as what God *is*. God being Eternality, Man has to be eternal. God being eternal, living, loving, conscious Mind, Man has to be eternally alive, eternally loving, eternally conscious, and eternally the Mind that *knows* what It *is*.

The eternal, birthless, deathless Christ is the eternal, deathless Man. *You are this Man. I am this Man. Everyone who exists is this Man.* The Christ is the *only* Man in existence. It is true that the Christ is not generally realized to be Man. However, when the genuine and only Nature of the Christ is known, we are aware that the Christ-Man is the *only* Man. This glorious revelation dissolves all illusions pertaining to a temporal man whose life is said to be confined to a period between the illusions called birth and death.

If the Christ-Man could be born, that aspect of God called Man would have to begin. But this is impossible because God is eternal and everlastingly complete. Without that aspect of Itself called Christ, or the Christ-Man, God would not be complete. An incomplete God is impossible. Thus, God, existing without that aspect of Itself called the Christ-Man, is impossible.

Man, the Christ, never departs from God by reason of being Man. God never ceases to be God by reason of being Man. An assumptive mortal can know nothing of God. Neither can God know any thing of an assumptive mortal. The Mind that is God can know nothing of illusions. An illusion, being nothing of itself, can know nothing of itself. Thus, the only Man that can know God is the Christ-Man, who is God being that specific aspect of Itself. The Bible is very specific on this point:

> No man hath seen God at any time; the only begotten Son, which is in the bosom of the Father, he hath declared him (John 1:18).

Jesus, the Christ-Man, was visible when these words were spoken. Yet John refers to him as being "in the bosom of the Father." If we did not understand this paradox, it would certainly seem contradictory. Yet this seeming contradiction is really a wonderful statement of Truth. Jesus, the Christ, had never left the Father, God. He was, and is, in God, even as God is in him. This is true because God *is* the Christ-Man, even as the Christ-Man is God. For this reason, it does not mean much to say that Man was *in* God.

Neither would it mean anything of spiritual significance to say that God was *in* Man.

It is true that "no man hath seen the Father." But it is also true that the Christ-Man hath seen, and does see, the Father. The Son *is* the Father, even as the Father *is* the Son. That aspect of God known as the Christ is God, even as God is that aspect of Himself known as the Christ. Just as surely as God knows Himself to be the Christ-Man, so it is that the Christ-Man knows Himself to be God.

No temporary illusion called man can know itself to be God. Neither can God know Itself to be a temporary illusion called man. But the Christ-Man does know Himself to be God, even as God knows Himself to be the Christ-Man. And the Christ-Man is the only Man in existence now and eternally. The Christ-Man is the Identity, the Being, the Body of Everyone.

It is well to realize that there are not two of you, one called man and the other called Man. There is but one of you, and this One is Man, or better said, the Christ-Man. The basis of dualism is the illusion that there is a born man, subject to all the so-called laws of human life and behavior. Once we *know* that no such man exists, we have obliterated the very root of all duality, and the glorious Christ-Man is realized to be our *only* Identity, our *only* Being, and our *only* Body.

How well Jesus knew, and knows, the eternality of the Christ-Man. As we happily consider the genuine meaning of Christmas, we can rejoice that we too know the eternality of the Christ-Identity, who exists as the Identity of each one of us. We know that Jesus' mission was not to save sinners or to heal bodies. Rather, it was, and is, the revelation of the eternal, birthless, deathless Nature of you, of me, and of everyone. We cannot rejoice at the so-called birth of One to whom birth was unknown, but we can rejoice in our sure knowledge that eternal Life is the *only*

Life that lives, that eternal Consciousness is the *only* Consciousness that is conscious, that eternal Love is the *only* Love that is loving, and that eternal Mind is the *only* Mind that is intelligent. Thus, we are rejoicing because you, I, and everyone in existence is eternal and ever complete in all ways. This is the true spiritual significance of Christmas. Let us rejoice that God so loves the world that He appears *as* Jesus the Christ and as the Christ-Man of each one of us.

The New Year

At the close of the Christmas holidays, we arrive at what is called the New Year. There is much celebration of this New Year, although there are few of us who really understand the tremendous spiritual significance behind this seemingly human event. It is paradoxical that the constant newness of Existence should be so inherent in and as our Consciousness that it even shows forth in what is called the human mind and experience. It is true that this inner awareness of Newness is generally misinterpreted and the so-called human misconception seems to conceal the genuine perception of this Truth. Even so, it is wonderful that even in the seemingly human scene there is at least some glimmer of Truth that shines through the darkest misperception.

If there were no inherent awareness that newness exists, there would be no recognition of it as being a possibility. Before any consideration of a fact can take place, there must be an awareness that this fact exists. In and as each one of us, there is the awareness that newness *is*. Thus, there is some consideration of newness. For instance, the New Year is welcomed with a sense of fresh hope and joy. New resolutions are made, and there is the hope that the New Year will bring happiness and well-being into our experience. Instinctively we know that joy, well-being, health, etc., do exist. If we did not know this to be true, we would have no hope of being permitted to experience these perfectly normal aspects of existence. It is noteworthy that the hope for better experiences is particularly allied to the New Year. Somehow peace, joy, health, prosperity, all that is normal, are allied to newness.

There are many ways in which the Truths of Existence are sensed and acted upon, even in the human scene of appearances. In former issues of *The Word*, we have mentioned that the space effort is due to our inherent awareness of freedom. If boundless freedom did not exist, there would be no effort to realize and experience this freedom. We know that we are boundless and immeasurable. We know that we are not bound to Earth and that we are not subject to nonexistent boundaries. Every so-called human desire for freedom is based upon the innate awareness of the fact that freedom is an established fact and that it is normal. If there were no such thing as freedom, there would be no striving for this normal experience.

Freedom *is*. Thus, we are aware that it exists. Always our mistake is that we imagine freedom to be a condition that must be *attained*. This is not the way of freedom. Actually, any effort to attain any goal can only seem to postpone that goal. It always seems to place the goal in the future, which does not exist. Then, too, if we feel that something must be attained, we are also accepting the fallacy that what we are seeking is absent now. Freedom *is*. Just as surely as we are aware of the fact that freedom exists, we are also aware that we are conscious of this fact. The only freedom there is eternally exists within and as the Consciousness of each and every Identity.

Freedom is but one of the innumerable aspects of Existence which is perceived, though dimly and imperfectly, in the very midst of this illusory appearance. All that is true of freedom is true of peace, joy, and every experience that we know to be good, perfect, and normal. Our point is that *only* because we inherently know that peace, joy, health, wholeness, abundance, etc., exist are these aspects of Existence included in our consideration of newness.

Throughout our Bible, we find references to newness. We find this same hope expressed in every Bible of the world. Why? Because newness is an eternally established fact, and even though we *seem* to seek for it or to attain it, it is already established within and as our own Consciousness.

> Remember ye not the former things, neither consider the things of old. Behold, I will do a new thing; now it shall spring forth; shall ye not know it? I will even make a way in the wilderness, and rivers in the desert (Isa. 43:18-19).

The first statement of this quotation is very revealing. It states clearly the reason why we *seem* to be burdened with "oldness." We seem to cling tenaciously to the accumulated illusions of a fallacious human past. In this way, we are apparently so burdened with so-called failures, mistakes, frustrations, etc., that our spiritual perception of the constant glory that is here and now appears to be dimmed. In this statement from Isaiah, we are urged to forget the former things. In other words, we should turn away from this whole fallacy of accumulated illusions.

Now, it is true that the dismissal of a human past seems to be almost impossible. There is the fallacy of human memory to be considered and the whole false fabric of past human experiences. But there is a way in which it is possible to extinguish every fabrication of past mistakes, frustrations, etc., and this is the way of enlightened, or illumined, Consciousness. It is as illumined Consciousness that we perceive the whole fallacy of birth, change, age, and death. This exposure of these illusions reveals why there is no human past to remember. It is important that we know why a human past is an impossibility. After all, we are intelligent because we are Intelligence Itself. Consequently, we must know *why* there is no human past if we are to know that there *is* no human past.

All that seems to be old is an accumulation of illusory human experiences. These fallacious experiences could only happen in the illusory world of birth and death. When we realize that there is no such world, we can also realize why we are not the victims of the falsities of this kind of world. When we know that there is no such thing as a "born" man, we can perceive why there can be no man who has accumulated innumerable human frustrations, experiences, failures, resentments, etc. Thus, we can perceive the fact that a memory of these fallacious experiences is completely fictitious. In other words, we know that there is no such man and no such mind. In this way, we can and do know why we cannot be victimized by a miasmic memory of a kind of mind that never existed.

The enlightened Consciousness, which is *your* Consciousness, is aware of being eternal and uninterrupted by birth or death. This same enlightened Consciousness is completely free from any fallacious accumulation of human beliefs or illusions. In this realization, there is newness. Let us again consider the second verse of our foregoing quotation:

> Behold, I will do a new thing, now it shall spring forth, shall ye not know it? I will even make a way in the wilderness, and rivers in the desert (Isa. 43:19).

This is no prophecy. This is no promise of some future good to come forth. This is a simple statement of the way things *are* right here and right now.

Who is the "I" that is to know all this Truth? Who is this "I" that seems to be confined in a wilderness of shadows dimming the Light? Who is this "I" that is capable of perceiving the true Existence right in the midst of the seeming wilderness? Who is this "I" that can see and experience abundant joy, peace, freedom, perfection right here and now? Who is this "I" that can perceive the way right through the seeming wilderness? Who is this "I" that does perceive completeness right where the desert seems to be? Beloved, *You are this I.* There is but one *I.* What other *I* could there be?

The ever new *I* is the *only I.* The New Year is *now*, this very moment. The New Year is every moment of your entire Existence. You consist of conscious, living, loving Mind. This is the ever new *I* that you *are*. Therefore, you are timeless, spaceless freedom, Joy, Peace, and uninterrupted Perfection. Because you are Consciousness, you *are* aware of being what you are and nothing else. The "new heaven" and the "new earth" are here and now. The new heaven and the new earth are in your own Consciousness because they are comprised of your own Consciousness. The illumined Consciousness you are is Heaven and Earth, and you know that Earth *is* Heaven right here and right now.

Looking neither forward nor backward, you stand as the eternal, conscious, ever joyous freshness and newness that you are. Boundless as joy and freedom, you greet your God-Self as each experience of your newness is revealed. This is *your* New Year, for you are always *new*.

Questions and Answers

Q: What is the spiritual significance of hearing? What is the purpose of the ear?

A: The spiritual significance of hearing is Consciousness. But Consciousness is the genuine signification of virtually every aspect of Existence. We should dwell increasingly with the word *Consciousness*.

It is said that we have five senses. Everything that comes into our experience is supposed to be judged by the reports of these five senses. Yet again and again, it has been proven that these so-called five senses often misjudge and falsely report.

The five assumptive senses must necessarily report falsely because they of themselves are false. An illusion can only see, hear, or seem to be aware of its own delusions. But an illusion is *nothing*. Furthermore, this "nothing" is never really known. There is no one in existence who is deluded. However, there *is* Something behind, or beyond, the illusion called the five senses. This Something is Consciousness, or Awareness.

In fact, there is but one Sense, and this one is Consciousness. Of course, Consciousness is active as various aspects of Itself. These aspects are innumerable. To speak of the five senses is to mistake the true meaning and function of infinite Consciousness. Even in so-called human parlance, we speak of a sixth sense. But there are so many functions of Consciousness that it would be impossible to number them.

Hearing definitely is an active aspect of Consciousness. But hearing is inseparable from the infinite variety of the functions of Consciousness. Hearing and seeing are but distinct aspects of the same Consciousness. It has been mistakenly believed that form could only be apparent visually. However, form can be heard as well as seen. All great music has form. There are definitely song forms. Then there are various other forms in which music appears, such as the sonata, the fugue, etc. Anyone who is trained in composition can hear the form of whatever composition he is hearing, singing, or playing.

All good poetry has form, and of course, all good literature has form. Much more could be said about the various ways in which form can be discerned. Right now, our purpose is to perceive the inseparability of Consciousness in the various aspects of Its activity.

Every Truth that is true as Vision is also true as Hearing. We know that the eye is not a material vehicle through which vision is strained. Neither is the ear a material vehicle through which hearing is strained. Hearing is a universal Existent. It exists everywhere and eternally. The ears do not consist of an illusion called matter. Rather, the very Substance of the ear is Consciousness—*and it is Consciousness that hears*. There can be no loss of hearing because there can be no loss of Consciousness. The Consciousness that comprises the Substance called the ear *is* the Consciousness that hears. Even as infinite Vision is inseparable, so it is that hearing is also inseparable. Hearing does not become divided into multitudes of "hearings."

There is one Hearing and there is One who hears. It has been said that the eyes of God are everywhere. It can also be said that the ears of God are everywhere. This is true because hearing is an infinite, eternal activity of universal, conscious, living Mind.

Q: I see the Body of Light around those who seem to be more spiritually illumined, and depending upon their illumination, it seems that the Light is brighter and greater. Sometimes I see only a rim of Light, even when I am aware of a greater Light around someone else at the same time. I know that you have said that seeing this Light was our illumination. Why, then, do we not see the Light of all people since each one has a Body of Light? Since it is all the same

Light, why does it seem greater around some people than others?

A: It is true that only illumined Consciousness can see the Body of Light. But it is also true that many factors enter into this seeing. In perhaps the most complete aspect of illumination, the Light may be so brilliant that it tends to conceal the delineation of the Body, and you do not actually see the form of the Body. Yet you are aware that the Body exists, even though at the moment it may not be apparent.

In one aspect of illumination, you may see what appears to be greater or lesser degrees of Light. The Light may constitute the entirety of the Body, or It may be seen around the Body. There may be two or more Identities seated side by side, and one of them will show forth as brilliant Light and the other may show forth as no Light at all.

In a situation such as this, the degree of Light we see as any specific Identity has to do with the Consciousness of the Identity himself. For instance, if one appears to be very troubled, fearful, or angry, the Body of Light might not be visible at all. It is as though any *seemingly* darkened consciousness acts as a covering that conceals the Body of Light. The various degrees in which we see the Body of Light seem to depend upon the various aspects of the one we are seeing and also upon the particular aspect of our own illumination.

However, do not be deceived or misled about this fact: there is no Body in existence other than the Body of Light. When you are aware of being fully illumined, every Body that is visible is seen to be a glorious, perfect, eternal, beautiful Body of Light. It is impossible to analyze illumination. But we can and do recognize the various ways in which we experience this wonderful living Light.

December 1963

The Living Christ

Oh, glorious, everlasting One,
Oh, thou who hast been called the Son,
We know thy loving Presence;
We know thou art the Essence
Of living, conscious, perfect Mind
For whom we searched, only to find
That Christ and Man are ever One;
The living Father *is* the Son.

E'en though the Christ may seem concealed,
The living Christ is now revealed
As perfect Man, who doth exist
Eternally, despite the mist
That seemed to hide the glorious Light
That shone throughout the seeming night;
Oh, birthless One, fore'er the same,
How wonderful, we too can claim
Thy Name—the living Christ.

Light and Love,
Marie S. Watts

January 1964

In the beginning was the Word, and the Word was with God, and the Word was God.

—John 1:1

Dear One,

I do not have words with which to express my great thanks to you for your many expressions of Love at the Christmas season. If it were possible, I would write to each one of you, telling you of my gratitude. One of the glorious aspects of Christmas is the unselfed Love that is revealed and evidenced. This is certainly God in action.

I have dwelt much in seclusion these last few weeks. Always, when some tremendous Truths are insisting upon being revealed, I am impelled to be very much alone and very quiet. During these quiet days and nights of silent listening, glorious revelations have been, and are being, experienced. It is utterly impossible to describe these illumined experiences, but my Heart yearns to share every revelation with you. One day the words will be revealed that will enable us to really "speak the Word," and it will be perceived.

Oh, beloved One, more and more it is apparent that:

> There is one (One) alone, and there is not a second; yea, he hath neither child nor brother (Eccles. 4:8).

Indeed, there is no second Life, no second Consciousness, Mind, and no second Love. The deceptive appearances of stolidity and solidity cannot deceive enlightened Mind. Right where darkness *seems* to be, there is Light. Vision infinite perceives things as they are. David, the Psalmist, gives us an inkling of the surging, flowing omniaction that is never evidenced in or as apparent darkness, solidity:

> What ailed thee, O thou sea, that thou fleddest? … Ye mountains, that ye skipped like rams; and ye little hills, like lambs? Tremble, thou earth, at the presence of the Lord … Which turned the rock into a standing water, the flint into a fountain of waters (Ps. 114:5-8).

There can be no doubt but that David perceived the glory, the freedom, the, joy, and the Beauty that is right here, right now. All seeming solidity, stolidity, and darkness were dissolved, as illumined Consciousness revealed the omni-active Omnipresence that *is* this Universe.

Somehow I feel impelled to call your attention to an article that appeared in one of the very early issues of *The Word*. The title of the article is "Omniaction," and you will find it in the April 1960 issue of *The Word* [*The Word 1960-1961* book—Ed.] At the moment, I do not know just why I am referring you to this article. But I do not question. I do know that it is of vital importance to realize that all activity is Omnipresence in action and that this realization should always be present in our contemplation. In any event, there is a purpose to be fulfilled by this article, "Omniaction," right now, and you will know why it has been called to your attention,

I must tell you how deeply I regret my inability to promptly answer your wonderful letters. Our Ultimate "family" is increasing so rapidly, and this means that the activities of the Ultimate are also rapidly increasing. I know you understand this, and my appreciation of your patience and understanding is indeed very great. Thank you more than I can say. Love alone is being evidenced as such loving consideration. The Love that you are is the Love that I am. Even as the Life, the Mind, the Consciousness that you are is the Life, the Mind, the Consciousness that I am. In all our "seeing" let us be aware that Love is the fire; Love is the Power of all that we know to be true.

This Is Life Eternal

> And this is life eternal, that they might know thee, the only true God, and Jesus Christ whom thou hast sent (John 17:3).

Life eternal, or eternal Life, consists of our knowledge that God is the *only* Life and that the Life that is God is eternal. But this is not all that is necessary if we are to really perceive the eternality of Life. We must also perceive that the eternal Life which is God is alive as the Life of everyone. We must realize that the *only* Life that is alive is eternal. God, eternal Life, was, and *is*, alive as the One called Jesus Christ. God, eternal Life, is also alive as the Life of the one called Mary, John, or whatever. Jesus knew that eternal Life was evidenced as his Life. We too must know that eternal Life is evidenced as our Life right here and now.

It is true that God is eternal Life. It is equally true that God is the *only* Life, but this will not help us much unless we realize that the God who is eternal Life is our *present* Life right here and right now.

Let us not be deceived. There really is but one Life. There is no such thing as the eternal Life that is God and another Life that is temporary. If there could be a temporal life, then the Life that is God would not be eternal. Thus, we would have a temporary God. This, of course, is ridiculous. But it is no more ridiculous than it is to believe that there is God, eternal Life, and another life that is born and must die. Eternal Life, by Its very nature, has to be everlasting Life. It cannot come into existence, neither can It go out of existence.

There are many supposititious fears rampant in the world of appearance. But the most general of all supposed fears, and perhaps the most hopeless of all, is the fear of death. Oh, there are many of us who will say we are not afraid of death. Perhaps we aren't afraid for ourselves, but few there are who are entirely free from the seeming fear of death for some loved one. The fear of death will be banished forever when we come to the point where we know, *really know*, that the *only* Life that is alive is God, eternal Life. But it is well to realize that in this happy experience there is also the sure, positive knowledge that there is no birth.

A prerequisite to the positive knowledge that Life eternal is the only Life that lives is the knowledge that Life is never born. Paradoxically, we seem to have been willing to accept the former Truth but strangely unwilling to accept the latter. It is impossible to know that Life is deathless unless we also know It is birthless. Once we have perceived the fallacy of birth, we are no longer concerned with death. Needless to say, this perception means the end of the so-called last enemy.

Jesus was well aware of the tendency to cling to a human sense of birth and all the things of the world that accompany this illusion. You will remember he said:

> He that loveth his life shall lose it; and he that hateth his life in this world shall keep it unto life eternal (John 12:25).

To love the supposed life in this world of appearance is to believe in and to accept everything pertaining to birth. To cling to this false concept of life means to believe in a life that begins and ends. The loss of this false concept of life is inevitable because it is supposed to have beginning, to be born. To believe in a temporal life would, of necessity, mean to live only temporarily. This is true because all there is of this supposititious life is the *mesmeric belief* in it. The supposed life in "this world" is not really Life at all. This fallacious belief of life and the believer in this kind of life are one. The belief and the believer are the same illusion, and the illusion is neither Life, Mind, nor Consciousness. Thus, there really is no belief in a temporal life, and neither is there a temporal life that is believed.

Actually, this illusory concept of life can never be lost. Anything that does not exist cannot be lost. All that can take place is the revelation of Life eternal, without beginning or ending. When the realization takes place that the foregoing facts are true, we are aware that this Life, that is alive as *our* Life, is eternal Life right now. It does not *become* eternal Life. It never stopped being everlasting. We have biblical authority for this statement:

> And this is the record, that God hath given to us eternal life, and this life is in his Son. He that hath the Son hath life; and he that hath not the Son of God hath not life (1 John 5:11-12).

Indeed, God hath given to us eternal Life. In Romans we read that the gift of God is eternal Life. The gift of God *is* God Itself. The gift of God is God being You. The gift of eternal Life *is* eternal Life. The gift of eternal Life is this Life being alive *as your Life* right here and now. The Father *is* the Son, even as the Son *is* the Father. The Life that is God is alive forevermore, and there is no other life to be alive.

When we know that we are Life eternal; we know that we have eternal Life. If we do not appear to realize that we *are* everlasting Life, we cannot appear to *have* everlasting Life. This is what Jesus meant when he said, "He that hath the Son hath life, and he that hath not the Son of God hath not life." If we do not know that eternal Life lives as our Life, we do not even know the meaning of Life Itself. How, then, can we consciously have, or experience, being Life eternal?

Right here, let us diverge for a moment. You will note that I have used many quotations from our Bible in this and many other articles and writings of the Ultimate. There is a definite purpose in the use of these quotations. I have read virtually all the religious or spiritual literature of the world, and I have found much Truth in all of them. I have also found much that I could not accept. But the point I wish to make is this: every Truth that I have found in any enlightened literature is stated right in our own beloved Bible.

It is true that our Bible contains statements which we cannot accept, but it is also true that every Truth we can read in any book may be found within the pages of our own Bible. However, we must know what we are seeking. We must recognize it when we see it. We must be sufficiently enlightened to perceive the Truth behind and beyond the sometimes misleading semantics of the statements. Once we are aware that God is All, All is God, we will find this Absolute Truth everywhere. This is particularly true of the writings in our Bible.

Now let us return to our subject, Life Eternal. We have discussed the fact that the only Life that is alive is eternal Life. We have perceived the fallacy of birth and death. Now let us explore the fictitious appearance that makes birth and death, a temporary life, seem so very real to us We are prepared to perceive the illusory nature of that which seems to be born and to die. It is the body that seems to be born. It is this same body that seems to die. Consequently, we must know what constitutes the Body if we are to perceive Life eternal.

It is futile to deny the existence of the Body. It is not intelligent to despise the Body. The belief, accepted by some faiths, that the Body must cease to live but that Life continues is fallacious. The generally accepted belief that Life, Consciousness, Soul enter the Body and thus must leave the Body would, if it were possible, be Self-destructive.

It is necessary to be aware of the eternal Body if we are to be aware of eternal Life. We must realize that the Body is as everlasting as is the Life. This is true because it is the Body that is the evidence of the presence of Life Itself. If the evidence of eternal Life must disappear, it would follow that Life would have to disappear. Thus, there would be no such thing as Life eternal. But Life *is* eternal, and Life's evidence of Itself is as eternal as is Life Itself.

No doubt it will occur to you that there is certainly some evidence of a body that is born. But what is this evidence? Who sees it? What mind knows it? What consciousness is aware of it? If the entire appearance of life in a world of materiality is illusion, the kind of body that appears to come into this illusory world must be included in the illusion. Thus, the evidence of a body that is born, a temporary body, must consist of the stuff of illusion. It is no more substantial than is the body that appears in the night dream. The very supposititious mind that *seems* to see and know a born body constitutes the supposed substance and activity of this seemingly born body. In other words, the illusion produces its own forms and activity from the illusory substance of itself. The illusory born body is not the evidence of eternal Life, Consciousness, Mind. Consequently, it is false evidence, thus, no genuine evidence at all.

Life is alive. Life, in order to be alive, has to be alive as Something. It is. It is alive as Its own evidence of Itself. It is alive as Its own embodiment of Itself. Thus, the Body of Life has to be as beginningless and as endless as is Life Itself. The eternal Body is alive eternally. It has to be this way because the eternal Body consists of eternal Life. There can be no unconscious Life. The *only* Life there is, is conscious Life. Thus, Consciousness is as eternal as is Life.

Consciousness and Life are inseparably One. There can be no inactive Life. Activity is the evidence that Life *is*. But activity must be perfect in order to be eternal. This perfect activity necessitates Mind, or Intelligence. Mind in action is perfect activity because it is *intelligent* activity. There is no way to separate Mind from Its intelligent activity. Mind, intelligently active, is omniactive Life Itself.

We know that Life is inseparable from Consciousness. So here we have arrived at the oneness of eternal Life, eternal Consciousness, and eternal Mind, or Intelligence. This, dear One, is *the eternal Substance of the eternal Body of Life*. It has been called a Body of Spirit. It has been called an immortal Body. But we must know, and we are in the process of discovering, what constitutes the Body we have called a spiritual Body. The eternality of Life cannot be fully realized until the eternality of *that which is alive* is known. It is the eternal Body that is eternally alive, and the Substance of the eternal Body is living, conscious Mind, or the inseparable Completeness that is God.

Of course, we cannot leave Love out of our consideration of the Body. Without Love, we would have nothing but cold intellectualism, and this would be nonintelligent indeed. Briefly stated, it is Love that maintains the complete, harmonious activity of the eternal Body. We have recently presented an article on this subject, Love, and we will not be repetitious, so suffice it to say that without Love there would be hate and anger, and this would very quickly destroy the Body. But there is no mind that hates or that acts hatefully or destructively.

If, to quote the poet Longfellow, "Dust thou art, to dust returnest, was not spoken of the Soul," neither was it spoken of the Body. The Body is as eternal as is the Soul because the Body *is* the living, intelligent, loving Soul, or Consciousness.

> And this is the promise that he hath promised us, even eternal life (1 John 2:25).

We are at the standpoint of the fulfillment of this promise. If we are ready to—and will—perceive the nothingness of birth, we can also perceive the nothingness of death. The promise of eternal Life must someday be realized. The evidence of the fulfillment of this promise must sometime be apparent.

Beloved, let us consider these tremendous Truths pertaining to the eternal Body of Life. In this way, we will be at least approaching the realization of the fulfillment of the promise. Inherently we *know* that Life is eternal. Let us accept the genuiness of that which lives eternally—the eternal Body.

Absolute Faith

Webster defines faith as "an act or state of acknowledging unquestioningly the existence, power, etc., of a supreme being, and the reality of a divine order."

This is quite a clear statement of the kind of faith that "moves mountains." You will note the word *unquestioningly* in the foregoing definition. There is only one kind of faith that can trust God implicitly and without questioning, and this is Absolute faith. But it is impossible to have Absolute faith unless there is Absolute knowledge. Absolute knowledge is an immovable awareness of the Truth, and the *only* Truth there is has to have Its basis in the fact that God is All, All is God.

Needless to say, there can be no dualism in Absolute faith. Such faith precludes the acceptance of *any* presence that is not God. Absolute faith cannot have one single element of doubt in it. The cry "Lord, I believe, help thou mine unbelief" (Mark 9:24) cannot enter into the faith that is Absolute.

Let us, for a moment, consider the record of the epileptic boy whom the disciples were unable to heal. You will recall that when Jesus was apprised of the situation, he cried out, "O faithless generation, how long shall I be with you?" (Mark 9:19). Here the inference is very plain. Jesus knew that the false evidence seemed overwhelming. He also knew that had the faith been Absolute, the perfection of the boy would have been apparent, and this perfection would have been evident right where the *false* evidence had seemed to be so real.

Jesus' Absolute faith was firmly based in his Absolute knowledge that God is All. The evidence of the rightness of his faith was apparent when the boy was perceived to be perfectly normal. The disciples must have been puzzled as to why the boy did not seem to respond to the Truth they knew. The record states that they asked him, "Why could not we cast him out?" In Jesus' answer to this question, we have the entire basis of Absolute faith:

> And he said unto them, This kind can come forth by nothing, but by prayer and fasting (Mark 9:29).

Jesus' prayer certainly was not a prayer in the orthodox sense of the word. His prayer was not based upon faith without knowledge. Rather, his faith had to be perfect faith because his knowledge was, and is, perfect knowledge. Absolute knowledge, completely free from duality, *is* perfect knowledge. Actually, Absolute knowledge is the *only* knowledge because the only Mind that can really know anything is the perfect Mind that is God.

Oh, I know, sometimes it *seems* almost impossible to keep our faith pure and Absolute. Sometimes the false evidence would overwhelm us if this were possible. Sometimes we may seem to waver between faith, belief, and unbelief. We too may be tempted to cry, "Lord, I believe, help thou mine unbelief." Yet we realize that we *must* somehow remain firm in our faith, and despite our apparent wavering, we do continue to turn and return repeatedly to our basic premise: God *is* All, All *is* God.

Please, dear One, be assured—we do reach a point beyond all wavering. We do arrive at that unshakable conviction that cannot be moved, no matter how convincing the false evidence may seem to be.

One of the most subtle arguments is that our knowledge is limited. We may be tempted to say, "But I know so little of Truth. I just can't depend upon my limited knowledge. I don't know enough." Right here it is well to realize that whatever knowledge is necessary at any given moment is sufficient for that moment and for that situation. But it is necessary to be sure that our knowledge is basically pure, Absolute. Even if it *seems* to us that we know very little, let us be certain that what we do know is firmly based in the fact that God is All.

Certain it is that we can perceive that God is the *only* Life, the *only* Consciousness, and the *only* Mind, or Intelligence. This is the basic Absolute Truth. But by this same token, we can also know that God is the *only* Presence; so All that is present *is* God. We can know that the *only* Presence, of necessity, is the *only* Power. This will lead us very quickly to realize that God, Omniaction, is the only activity and the only Presence and Power that is active. Any perception that is based in Absolute Truth inevitably brings greater revelation. The essential requisite is that we remain firmly established in our Absolute basis: God is All.

You will note that Jesus used the word *fasting* in the foregoing quotation. Generally speaking, to fast means to voluntarily abstain from the partaking of food. Fasting as a religious rite is supposed to be temporary, and it may be only an abstinence from eating meat. But Jesus' use of the word *fasting* had a much deeper and more spiritual meaning than merely an abstinence from food. Let us explore the genuine spiritual significance of his use of this word.

We know Jesus realized that enlightenment was not at all dependent on a total or partial abstinence from food. Yet the very word *fasting* reveals that he did realize the necessity to abstain from something. Indeed, it is necessary to entirely abstain from a fallacious appearance of materiality. It is essential that we refuse to accept, or take in, any seeming appearance of inharmony or imperfection. It is imperative that we abstain from anything and everything that is not based entirely in the fact that God is All, All is God. This abstinence cannot be partial. Neither can it be temporary. There must be a constant, uninterrupted awareness of the Allness and the Onliness of God.

There is not a one of us who is not daily faced with fallacious evidence. This pretense to existence may sometimes *appear* very real and formidable. Yet if we are constantly abiding in the Absolute fact, God is All, false evidence does not deceive us. Neither does it disturb us. Our Absolute faith remains intact and invulnerable.

When our faith is Absolute, we do not question as to why some inharmony has appeared. We do not speculate upon what it is or might be. Neither do we wonder what caused it. We simply know it isn't. We do not argue with it or about it.

We do not honor it as either cause or effect. We know, without trying to know, that there is no cause and effect. We know this is impossible because our knowledge is Absolute. We realize that the Allness, the Onliness, the Nowness, and the Hereness of God preclude the possibility of cause and effect. In other words, we know why there can be no inharmony. We know why there can be no cause and effect. This is the basis of our Absolute faith.

God is Perfection. God is All. So All is Perfection. Faith in God is faith in Perfection. Faith in the All-Presence of God is faith in the All-Presence of Perfection. This means that we perceive no presence other than Perfection. Faith in Perfection cannot be conditioned faith. Neither can it be qualified. It cannot be tempered with faith in imperfection. It is impossible to have Absolute faith in omnipresent Perfection and yet have some faith in imperfection. It has to be Absolute faith, based in Absolute knowledge.

Dear One, do not criticize yourself if you seem to waver in your faith. Don't condemn yourself if it seems to fluctuate. Don't be discouraged if it sometimes seems weak and uncertain. Please know that all of us have seemed to travel this same rocky road. Self-condemnation serves no purpose. It is futile, and it can only seem to delay that happy day when you realize constant Absolute faith.

If you seem to falter, know that all of us have seemed to falter. Just open your Eyes, spiritual vision, a little wider. Lift your vision, spiritual awareness, a little higher. Make no effort. Remember, Jesus did not tell anyone to read a book or get a lesson in order to be whole. He simply said, "I will; be thou clean" (Matt. 8:3).

Thus it is with us. Just abide as constantly as possible in the basic Absolute Truth—God is All, All is God. You will find your faith becoming more Absolute and more constant. You will find the temptations to doubt or to waver are not so frequent or so severe. It does help sometimes to realize that *only* because God is the Allness of you, can you be or exist. It is sometimes good to remind yourself that your Life is God living, your Mind is God knowing, and your Consciousness is God being conscious. However, don't work at it. Just consider it as an established fact. Consider it as you would view the Beauty of a scene, the surging flow of the tides, or the glory of the stars.

There is great calmness and serenity in the contemplation of the Allness of God. But there is also intense, active joy in this contemplation. Let God, who really is your Consciousness, be conscious *as* you. Nothing can stop God. Nothing can keep Consciousness from being conscious. Actually, there is nothing in existence that can in any way oppose, obstruct, or delay God being all.

The Mind that is God is intelligent as your entire Life right now. The Consciousness that is God is conscious as your Consciousness right now. This is true. This is all that *is* true. This is Absolute Truth. This is what *you are.*

Questions and Answers

Q: Here is a point that I can't seem to receive Light on. You say, "It is never a getting rid of a false sense of identity. Rather, it is a seeing through a mistaken concept of Identity, enabling the "I" that I am to emerge. Who has to see through it? Who has this mistaken concept? If the One and only "I" that I am is untouched and unaffected and unconcerned with the fantasy, who then has to see through it? There are not two of us.

A: This is a deeply penetrative question, and only those of you who are greatly enlightened would ask questions such as this.

I have used the expression *see through* in my writings. I do not recall having used the word *emerge*, although it is possible that this quotation is correct. As I have often stated, words are such tricky things. They are such inadequate instruments to use in speaking or writing of the deep Truths of God. Nevertheless, words are what we have, and words are what we must use for right now. There will come a day when words are no longer necessary, and that will be a happy day indeed.

Now, let us consider the question that was asked. Actually, the expression *see through*, in this instance, can be misleading. It implies the presence of something false to be seen through and an assumptive identity to see through the falsity. The genuine and *only* Identity can never really "emerge." Always It has existed, and forever It will continue to exist. It is true, however, that we do not always *seem* to be fully aware of *being* the eternal God identified, or the God-Identity.

As stated in *You Are the Splendor*, all of us have experienced some aspects of illumined Consciousness. There is one aspect of illumination in which things that had appeared solid are seen and known to be completely transparent. We do not actually "see through" the apparent solidity. We know that no solidity exists to be seen through. It is as though our Consciousness suddenly clarifies, and things are seen as they are and as they have always been. We do not change from one Identity to another in this experience. Rather, it is the eternal Identity clearly perceiving Existence as It is.

This one and only Identity is never really aware of density or solidity. Never has It been touched by darkness or ignorance. Never was It deceived by it. The sun knows nothing of the clouds that sometimes seem to hide it from our vision. It just goes right on being what it is and shining as its own Light. The clouds are not *in* the sun, and the sun is not *in* the clouds. It never occurs to us that the sun has vanished just because we do not see it or its light for a moment. We just know that the sun continues to exist. There may not seem to be any evidence of its existence, but we are not deceived.

Thus it is with our eternal Identity. Inherently we know that we exist. This is true because we are *conscious* of being and of being an Identity. Our awareness, Consciousness, of being is never touched by any ignorance of what we genuinely are. Ignorance is unknown to the Mind that we are. Yet ignorance, darkness, can *seem* to temporarily hide or conceal the Light we know our Self to be. But we go right on shining. We go right on knowing what we are.

It is not a matter of "seeing through" something that does not exist. Rather, it is being conscious of that which does exist. It is the certain knowledge of being an eternal, perfect God-Identity, whether or not the visible evidence of this fact appears to be apparent at the moment. When this knowledge is firm enough and sure enough, the Body of Light is evident. But this is not all. That which had appeared dense and solid is no longer apparent, and all Existence is seen to be living, perfect Light.

It is an awareness of Truth, even though the evidence *seems* to be quite contrary to that which we *know* to be true. As we continue to know that which is true, without effort, the evidence of the Truth we know is seen, known, and experienced. When we know, really know, that which is true, no false evidence disturbs us. We are completely invulnerable. We are just as sure of the rightness of what we know as we are that the sun is right here, shining away, even though we do not at the moment see it.

This, Dear One, is just what is meant by "seeing through" any false evidence. It is simply the conscious, living Mind you are, refusing to be deceived.

Love Doth Abide

The whispering grass, the rustling leaves,
The singing wind among the trees,
In ecstasy sublime
Declare I am Divine;
The glorious Beauty of the rose,
Reaches the Heart of one who knows
That Beauty, Love, and Life
Abide, right where the strife
Of angry men may seem to be;
Oh! God is here, for all to see.

No matter though the world seem blind,
Though cruelty appears to bind
The Heart and Soul of men,
They shall awake again
To see that Life and Love endure,
That Man forevermore is pure,
And free from hate and fear;
Man knows that Love is here
In every clime, in every land,
E'en glowing in the Heart of Man.

Light and Love,
Marie S. Watts

February 1964

In the beginning was the Word, and the Word was with God, and the Word was God.

—John 1:1

Dear One,

Spring is in the air here in Vista, and there is a wonderful sense of freshness and newness. The view from my study window is so inspiring.

In the foreground there is a large green shrub, literally laded with bright red berries. Just back of this Christmassy shrub, there is a huge palm tree, with branches gently, rhythmically swaying in the breeze. Right next to this stately palm tree, there stands a beautiful jacaranda tree. Fresh new leaves in various shades of green are garmenting this tree for the spring and summer wearing.

In the background are the hills, dotted with houses of various colors. Then there are the trees of the groves, marching up and down the hillsides. Beyond all of this Beauty, there are the seemingly distant mountains, in purples, lavenders, several shades of pink, and a fairy-like mist of golden-colored Light.

All of this I see in form and I know that it exists. But I also know that the Substance of all this Beauty in form is Consciousness. I am keenly aware that the Substance in form I am seeing is no more dense than is the blue, blue sky or the snow-white clouds playing hide and seek in the heavens.

As this marvelous Universe of Light is seen and experienced, my Heart sings a joyous song of gratitude. Isn't it wonderful that, right in the midst of a world that seems to be in such turmoil, we can and do perceive this Heaven and this Earth as the very Substance of God made evident? This World, right here and right now, *is* Heaven. Though pretentious power-mad little men may not know this to be true, we know it is true. The "little men" must and will awake. Let us be sure we do not fall asleep beside them.

Oh, I know, sometimes our Hearts cry out. Sometimes we long to take the whole world in our arms of Love and say, "Beloved, awaken; just open your Eyes and *see*. This is the way it *is*." Yet we know that God, the One Consciousness of All of us, is lovingly and intelligently fulfilling Its purpose, and we must not be concerned.

However, we are not helpless. We can be fulfilling the purpose of our seeing. Furthermore, we can know that the activity of our seeing is fraught with power. We do know that our seeing is unconfined and that it is not limited in *any* way. We do know that the Truth we are conscious of seeing and being this moment is equally present, active, and conscious in, through, and as the Consciousness of everyone, everywhere. Despite any appearance to the contrary, God, the *only* Consciousness, is indivisibly One. So we just go right on with our seeing. We continue to *be* the Light we are seeing. In this way, we can be assured that we *are* the Light of the World. After all, this is our only purpose in being.

Now I must try, with inadequate words, to thank you. An exceptional number of you have written letters of pure, joyous gratitude for *The Word* of last month, January. You say that the revelations in this latest *Word* are greater than ever before. Yes, indeed this is true. But dear One, if *you* were not more enlightened than ever before, *you would not recognize* these higher revelations. They are really *your* revelations.

Some of you have even written that you were experiencing revelations of the very same Truths which were presented in the January issue of *The Word*. Thus, you see, no revelation is limited to the Consciousness of either the revelator or to the one who reads the words in which it is revealed. Every Truth you realize is *your* revelation. You are the revelator of every Truth you perceive. This revelation would occur as your Consciousness, whether or not you read it in words.

Nonetheless, it is inspiring and helpful to read the words of our revelations. Sometimes just seeing it in print tends to crystalize it for us. Sometimes we may be more consciously aware of the Truth that has been revealed, just through reading this Truth expressed, as well as is possible, in words.

With this issue of *The Word*, we have arrived at the close of our fourth year of this joyous activity.

Now it can be told: I was reluctant to begin publication of *The Word*. Months before the first issue of *The Word* was published, I sensed that this must be done. Yet I resisted taking the step. As you know, I have never wanted any personal element to enter into the activity of the Ultimate. Above all, I did not want a monthly publication to be a personal message from an assumptive leader to followers who believed that they were limited. However, one evening the title for this activity was clearly revealed; this title was so impersonal that all my reluctance dissolved, and *The Word has* been an impersonal monthly message of Truth.

I cannot tell you in words how happy I have been, and am, in this activity. Never will I be able to adequately express my gratitude for your many expressions of Love for *The Word* and joy in its contemplation.

The Burning Bush

> Now Moses kept the flock of Jethro his father-in-law … and he led the flock to the backside of the desert, and came to the mountain of God, even to **Horeb.**

> And the angel of the Lord appeared to him in a flame of fire out of the midst of a bush: and he looked, and, behold, the bush burned with fire, and the bush was not consumed.
>
> And Moses said, I will now turn aside, and see this great sight, why the bush is not burnt (Exod. 3:1-3).

Perhaps there is no episode in the Bible that is more fraught with spiritual significance as is the foregoing experience of Moses and the burning bush that did not burn.

It is noteworthy that it took the fire to attract Moses' attention to the bush. It is also worth noting that, had the bush actually been in the process of destruction by fire, Moses would not have turned aside to investigate what was taking place. It was the paradox of the burning bush that was not being consumed that alerted Moses to the presence of Something that was necessary for him to perceive and to understand.

Suppose Moses had not turned aside to investigate this phenomenon. Suppose he had just closed his eyes, Consciousness, and said, "Well, I must be having hallucinations. If that bush is on fire, it has to be actually destroyed by fire." Or suppose Moses had just ignored the whole appearance. Had he done any of these things, the children of Israel might not have been led out of bondage to the Egyptians.

But Moses did heed the signal, and this is exactly why the fire appeared. It was the *signal* to attract the attention of Moses. Although the fire *appeared* to be a destructive presence, it was really a signal signifying the presence of God. The fire, destructive element, was not real. It had no actual existence. But God, signified by the fire, was and is genuine.

Moses didn't try to put out the fire. He didn't try to do anything about the fire. He did not run away from it; he was not afraid of it. He investigated it. He turned aside from his path in order to determine why the fire should be evident in the bush, but yet the bush did not burn. And what did he find? He found God. He found the Presence that had been present right there, all the while.

> And when the Lord saw that he turned aside to see, God called unto him out of the midst of the bush, and said, Moses, Moses. And he said, Here am I. And he said, Draw not nigh hither: put off thy shoes from off thy feet, for the place whereon thou standest is holy ground (Exod. 3:4-5).

Yes, right where the destructive appearance of fire *seemed* to be, there was God. Remember, the Bible states that God called to Moses from the very midst of the burning bush.

The "holy ground" upon which Moses stood was the *whole, absolute, pure Truth.* It was the Wholeness, Oneness, Allness, and Entirety that is the *only* Substance—and this is God. Holy Ground denotes the Substance that is God and God alone. Holy Ground is the Consciousness that is aware of nothing other than of being this Substance. Apparently Moses had not seemed to be aware that he was standing on Holy Ground. In other words, it seemed he had not been aware that God *is* All, All *is* God. Well, this is the way it has *seemed* with most of us until we began to discover the glorious fact of the Allness of God.

There are many Truths of great spiritual significance in this episode of the burning bush that did not burn. For instance, although there was every appearance of fire, a destructive element, the Substance of that bush was not in the process of being destroyed. The Substance of the bush was never touched by the appearance of fire. It could not be consumed because it was comprised of eternal Consciousness, Spirit.

It symbolizes the eternal, immutable, indestructible Substance which is the *only* Substance in existence. It represents the Substance of you, of me, and of everyone. The indestructible, imperishable, eternal Substance which constitutes your Body and mine is never penetrated or invaded by any destructive *appearance*, No matter how threatening some false evidence may seem to be or how real it may seem, the Substance of the Body remains immune to and untouched by the fallacious evidence.

It is always *false* evidence. This means that it is not evidence of anything genuine or real. Actually, it is evidence of "nothing" or "no thing," thus, it is no evidence at all. When once we know, *really* know, the nature of all Substance, we are no longer deceived by fallacious evidenced We cannot be deluded by it, and we cannot fear it. We just *know*, and nothing can convince us that there is any substance other than God being *that* Substance.

False evidence cannot deceive or disturb anyone who knows that which is true. One who knows, *and knows that he knows*, never seeks to find a cause for fallacious evidence. He never asks, "Why did this happen to me?" or "What is the cause of this?" He never concerns himself with its *apparent* substance or activity. He is totally unconcerned with the false evidence. He is wholly and completely convinced of the nothingness of an imperfect appearance, and he is concerned only with the genuine and only Substance and activity which does exist.

It is true that all of us are sometimes faced with some seeming evidence of imperfection. There is a tendency to seek a cause for this appearance of nothing. There is also the temptation to ask why this should have appeared in our experience, when we were being so faithful and sincere in our reading and contemplation.

Such questioning can only *seem* to delay our realization and the evidence of the Truth we *know* to be true. You see, to concern ourselves with the fallacious appearance, in any way, is to honor it as something. Thus, it can *seem* to continue to be present and to have power to deceive us. There can be no power unless there is presence. *Anything that is not present cannot be power.* There is no evil presence because God is *All Presence*. Consequently, there can be no evil power. God alone is the Presence, and God alone is the Power.

This brings me back to the fire in the midst of the burning bush. What was that fire? Was it evil? Where and what was the evil that attracted Moses' attention? Obviously it was not a destructive presence. It was neither an evil substance nor an evil activity. Therefore, the fire was not evil. In other words, the fire was not what it seemed to be.

In orthodoxy, we were taught that trouble or inharmony of any kind was sent as a punishment for wrongdoing. In metaphysics, we were told that these evil appearances were due to wrong thinking. Actually, neither of these conclusions can be true. God really *is* All, and this precludes the possibility of *any* evil. No matter under what guise it may appear, evil simply does not exist. Therefore, anything that appears to be evil cannot be what it appears to be. It can only seem to be evil if we decide that something evil is present and has power.

Actually, there is no false evidence. The only thing false about any evidence is our misinterpretation of that which is already perfect, right here and now. The signal which signifies the Presence of God is not false evidence. Yet it can seem to be false evidence to us if we do not understand it and consider it to be imperfection or an evil presence of any nature. That which we have called false evidence is really our misinterpretation of the perfect evidence which can never be displaced or obliterated. For the purpose of clarity, we do speak of false evidence. But don't be deceived. The *only* evidence in existence is perfect evidence. It has to be perfect because God is all there is to be evidenced.

Always remember, "The place whereon thou standest is holy ground." Right where you are, there is God and God alone. But this is not all. *God is what you are.* Your Body cannot be left out of what you *are*. If something should appear that seems to be evil, be assured that it cannot be what it seems to be. Rightly perceived, it is but a signal, drawing your attention to the Good, God, that is the entirety of your Being and Body.

You will not misinterpret the signal. You will not be deceived. You will not imagine that this signal signifies evil, trouble, danger, or anything other than God. Right where the signal appears, there is God, and God is All that can be present. No matter how frightening any apparent false evidence may seem to be, you will stand firmly in your awareness that God is the *only* Presence; God is the *only* Power that is present; and God is wholly and entirely Good, perfect, and eternal. Furthermore, God is a constant Existent, without change and without interruption—and this, beloved One, is what you are, right here and right now.

Absolute Truth

There seems to have been some controversy between students of metaphysics and students of the Absolute. There are those who feel that the Absolute is just *too* absolute for them. They seem to find it necessary to do "mental work," and they are very sincere about this matter.

We have no quarrel with those who feel the necessity for a dualistic approach. However, there is one fact that must be realized sooner or later by each and every one of us: *every Truth is an Absolute Truth.* No Truth can be partially true. No Truth can be a qualified Truth. No Truth can be a temporary Truth, and neither can It be a "sometimes" Truth,

Truth is that which is true, genuine, real. Every Truth is a universal Truth. Every Truth is an eternal Truth. Every Truth is a constant, uninterrupted Truth. Actually, Truth is a universal Constant. Whenever we say, "God is All, All is God," we have stated a universal, constant fact. When we say, "God is the only Life, Substance, Intelligence, Consciousness, Love, and Activity," we have stated a universal, constant fact.

We cannot qualify these facts by doing mental work to try to make a universal, constant fact be any more true or any more present than It already is. We cannot bring any Truth into existence. We can never use the Truth. Truth is Its own activity. We cannot make Truth be any more present or active than It eternally is.

Of course, this does not mean that students of the Absolute are inactive. Quite the contrary is true. We are intensely active. But our activity is not one of mental work. It certainly is not an effort to *use* the Truth. Truth is God, and how can anyone use God? We do not try to bring Truth into existence. No, not even in our own affairs do we try to make Truth active. We know that Truth is omnipresent, and we know that there is nothing present that is not true.

Our activity is one of contemplation. We actively contemplate the universal, constant Truths that constitute this Universe. We permit no illusory falsity to deceive us. We take no mental detours. We make no affirmations and denials. Neither do we mentally drift like a cloud in the sky.

Our activity in contemplation is the Truth in action. We do not bring this Truth into activity by our contemplation. Always, Truth is active. However, when we contemplate, we are actively aware of the Truth in action. But this is not all. We are also aware of *being* the Truth in action. This has nothing to do with affirmation and denial. It has nothing to do with a method or formula. It is not a treatment.

Our activity in contemplation is a calm, peaceful, joyous consideration of the Truth that already exists, and we are aware of It. The word *consider* is quite revealing in explaining what it means to contemplate. When we *consider* any fact, we know that the fact exists. We are not attempting to bring the fact into existence. We are not even trying to make it evident. We know the fact exists; we know it is already in evidence. Consequently, we simply consider the fact.

There may be many aspects of any fact. We may consider every aspect of any fact. Perhaps one aspect of a fact may seem more important than another in our consideration. This does not mean that one aspect of Truth is more important than another aspect. It is just that our attention may be focused more intently upon one particular aspect of Truth than upon another.

Let us clarify the foregoing paragraph. Suppose, for instance, that a threat to life seems imminent. If this should be the case, our attention would be focused on the Truth that is Life. Life is a universal Constant, and *this fact is the Truth.* Life is an eternal fact, or Truth. Life is without beginning, without change, and without ending. Life is unopposed. It is irresistible and irrepressible. There is nothing in existence to resist Life. Neither is there anything existing that can obstruct It, end It, or interfere with It in any way. Life simply *is*. It is, because It is a universal Constant. A universal Constant is a universal Truth.

We may consider Life in an infinite variety of aspects of Itself. We may consider the indivisible Nature of Life, or we may consider the ever newness of eternal Life. Oh, there are innumerable aspects of Life that may enter into our contemplation. Of one fact we may be assured: *the omnipotent Omnipresence that is Life will certainly be uppermost in our consideration.* No matter what aspect of Life comes to our attention, the Presence of the Power of Life, the Power of the Presence of Life, will be ever-present in and as our consideration. Needless to say, the word *death* does not even occur to us. What have we to do with that deception? We are concerned *only* with Life.

Now, Life is no more a universal, constant fact than is Consciousness. As we know, Life and Consciousness are inseparably One. Thus, the Truth that is Consciousness may be very important right here. We know that every fact that is true as Life is also true as Consciousness. We may find ourselves contemplating conscious Life or living Consciousness. Even so, we know that conscious Life is inseparable from Mind, or Intelligence. Mind knows what It is, and Consciousness is aware of *being* what It knows. Life is the knowing and the Being. Oh, we may contemplate more aspects of the Truth that is Life than we mention. In all our contemplation, we have been realizing the Absolute Truth. *This is the important fact that we must maintain.*

Of course, there are many ways in which our attention may be drawn to some specific aspect of Absolute Truth. For instance, there may be some appearance of lack and limitation. We are not going to be concerned with the "fire" that turns our attention to infinite Supply. We are only concerned with that aspect of Truth which is Supply. Completeness is a universal Constant; thus, completeness is a universal, absolute Fact. All Substance is complete Substance; all Intelligence is complete Intelligence; all Consciousness is complete Consciousness.

Conscious, living Mind is Its own uninterrupted maintenance and sustenance. It is Its own constant Supply. It is Its own awareness of *being* constantly complete. If a seeming lack of any kind attracts our attention to Supply, we may consider innumerable aspects in which Supply is present and evident. This is no formula. It is the Absolute Truth in action.

Sometimes there seems to be a tendency to consider Truth as something outside Itself, or other than, the one who is in contemplation. Actually, this is impossible because no one can consider any Truth that is other than his own Identity. Yet it is this false tendency that seems to separate Truth from the one who knows the Truth. The Bible says, "Every city or house divided against itself shall not stand" (Matt. 12:25). To know the Absolute Truth is to *be* the Absolute Truth you are knowing. You cannot be something outside of, or other than, your Self. Even as Jesus said, you know that you *are* the Truth.

You are the Absolute Truth. This Truth is not something that is true *about* you. It is not just something that is true *of* you. It is the Truth that is true *as* you and as All there is of your Entirety. Your dictionary will tell you that the word *Absolute* means free from imperfection, complete, free, perfect, free from mixture, whole, pure. This is what *you* are. This is the Absolute Truth you are. It is not something that may or may not be true *about* you. Beloved, it *is* you. It is your entire Life, Mind, Consciousness, Being, and Body. This Absolute Truth is true *as* you. It is true *as* your Life, *as* your Intelligence, *as* your Consciousness, *as* your Body. Above all, it is true *as* the Love that you are.

Never do we divide our attention between that which is true and that which is not true. Never do we misinterpret any signal that attracts our attention to some Absolute Truth. Neither do we ignore the signal. We recognize it. We accept it for just what it means, and we consider the Absolute Truth to which our attention has been drawn. There can be no halfway measure for us. There can be no hedging between the Absolute Truth which *is* and a partial or qualified truth which *is not*. We cannot be diverted from our Absolute seeing and Being. This is where we stand, and we can do no other.

Jesus knew what he meant when he said, "I am the truth." Beloved, you too know what you mean when you say, "I am the Truth." There is no Truth that is not Absolute Truth. When you say, "I am the Truth," you have really said, "I am Absolute Truth." This means you have said, "I am free from imperfection. I am complete. I am perfect. I am free from mixture. I am whole, and I am pure," Oh, yes, you can truly say, "I am the Absolute Truth," for this is what you *are*.

Now, you may find your Self saying something like this:

> I am the Absolute, perfect, changeless Truth. I am the universal, uninterrupted, constant Absolute Truth, for I am that I AM. I am the eternal, constant Absolute Truth, for I am that I AM. Perfection is a universal Absolute Truth, and I am that Truth. Perfection is an eternal, constant Absolute Truth, and I am that Truth.
>
> Life is an eternal, universal Absolute Truth, and I am that Truth. Infinite Intelligence is an eternal, universal, constant Absolute Truth, and I am that. Consciousness is an eternal, constant Absolute Truth, and I am that Truth.
>
> Love is an eternal, universal, uninterrupted Absolute Truth, and I am that Absolute Love. Light is an eternal, universal, constant Absolute Truth, and I am that true Light.

Oh, there are countless ways in which to say, "I am the Truth." No method or formula can be given for this God-experience. Beloved, let your own Consciousness reveal Itself *as* the absolute Truth that *you are*. Let your own glorious God-Self make Its own statements in Its own words. You are every absolute Truth in existence. Therefore, let the absolute Truth that you are announce Itself in Its own way. There is but one thing that is of the utmost importance, and this is the fact that *you are the absolute Truth and nothing else.*

Questions and Answers

Q: Is it necessary to experience illumination in order to be healed?

A: Of course, all of us know that never is there anything in need of healing. Yet we do have to use words, and perhaps the word *healed* is only another way of saying *Perfection evidenced.* In any event, let us explore this question.

Actually, there is no one who is not illumined, or enlightened, Consciousness. Our new book, *You Are the Splendor*, makes this fact very clear. God, Consciousness, is the *only* Consciousness and the *only One who is conscious.* Thus, it would be impossible to be conscious if one were not illumined Consciousness. This is true because God is Light. Nevertheless, it does seem that we are not generally aware of being illumined Consciousness. Then too, there are various aspects of illumination, and every one of us is aware of one or another aspect of this glorious, enlightened Consciousness.

In order to perceive the evidence of Perfection in any situation, it certainly is not necessary to experience that illumination which reveals your completeness as this Universe. There have been countless so-called healings when there seemed to be no awareness of being the Light at all. We know this to be true. We also know that many of those who experience "healing" go right on in their seeming darkness. The mere fact of healing does not necessarily mean a full or conscious awareness of being the Light.

There is a point, though, that is of some importance. Sooner or later, every one of us must experience *being* illumined Consciousness. But we will never experience this glorious Reality by denying that already we *are* the one and only enlightened Consciousness which is God. Of course, it may not seem to be possible at the moment. Nonetheless, it is true.

Let us have a simile here. If the body seems to be ill or imperfect, the perfect Body does not seem to be apparent. Yet we do not doubt the presence of the perfect Body, even though It may not seem to be evident at the moment. Our admission of the absolute fact that the Body is perfect right here and now is necessary in order that the Body of Perfection may be evident.

In this same way, we can admit the fact that we *are* illumined Consciousness. Although it may not seem to be evident at the moment, we should not deny the fact that we have to be illumined Consciousness in order to be conscious. Presently, if we do not struggle over it, our illumined Consciousness is evidenced, and then we know that *always* we have been this Consciousness.

Sometimes it seems we are too concerned about illumination. I know that all of us are eager for this glorious experience. But illumination alone does not guarantee the end of all our seeming difficulties. Illumination has been going on through the centuries, yet the illumined ones have continued to seem to suffer and to die. But this could never be if those who experienced illumination knew what it meant, what it signified. We cannot go into this aspect of illumination right now, but there is much that can be revealed pertaining to it.

When we reach the point of "walking around in the dream awake," we are walking as illumined Beings. This is the point beyond all appearance of sickness, suffering, age, trouble, or death. But we cannot hurry this experience. It comes as it will, and no one can determine its coming. In the meantime, it is well to know that whatever Truth is necessary at any moment is present, and it is sufficient for what seems to be the need of the moment. If we seem to be striving for more of Truth, if we seem to be struggling for illumination, we are not experiencing that perfect peace that is necessary to the revelation and evidence of omnipresent Perfection.

It is true that the ultimate enlightenment is constantly illumined Consciousness. It is also true that each one of us eagerly anticipates this joyous, peaceful, constant experience. Yet we should never be overanxious about this or anything else. Every student of the Absolute may rest assured that he will consciously experience illumination. It is inevitable because to study and contemplate the Absolute means that the Consciousness is already aware of some aspects of enlightened Consciousness. If we accept the fact that we *are* illumined Consciousness, even though we may not be fully aware of this fact, we will suddenly discover that we *really are* illumined, and we will see and experience the evidence of this fact.

Let us not concern ourselves with the how or the when of our conscious Illumination. Rather, let us go calmly on, rejoicing in the presence of that which we know to be Truth, even though it may not be completely evident at the moment. It *is* here, you know—and it is here right now.

Just as surely as you exist, the full, illumined Consciousness is here and now. You see, It is your own God-Consciousness.

February 1964

Love's Presence

'Tis Love that is alive
As every flower and tree;
'Tis Love that does not strive
In order that it be
Its perfect, glorious Self.

Oh, wondrous, perfect, living Love,
Omnipotence, so far above
All strife, all hate, all pain;
Thy Presence doth remain
Throughout Eternity.

The surging, flowing, beauteous Light
That glows throughout the darkest night
Is tender, gentle, living Love,
As calm and peaceful as the dove
Who represents all peace.

Love frees and blesses all
Who listen for its call,
And when our freedom is revealed,
E'en though it *seems* that we are healed,
'Tis but Love's Presence realized.

Light and Love,
Marie S. Watts

About the Author

During early childhood, Marie Watts began questioning: "Why am I? What am I? Where is God? What is God?"

After experiencing her first illumination at seven years of age, her hunger for the answers to these questions became intensified. Although she became a concert pianist, her search for the answers continued, leading her to study all religions, including those of the East.

Finally, ill and unsatisfied, she gave up her profession of music, discarded all books of ancient and modern religions, kept only the Bible, and went into virtual seclusion from the world for some eight years. It was out of the revelations and illuminations she experienced during those years, revelations that were sometimes the very opposite of what she had hitherto believed, that her own healing was realized.

During all the previous years, she had been active in helping others. After 1957, she devoted herself exclusively to the continuance of this healing work and to lecturing and teaching. Revelations continually came to her, and these have been set forth in this and every book.

To all seekers for Truth, for God, for an understanding of their own true Being, the words in her books will speak to your soul.